Thank You God

Thank You GOD

Finding Gratitude in Hard Times

R Lindemann

Aleph Publications
Wisconsin, USA

Thank You God
Finding Gratitude in Hard Times
Copyright 2019 - R Lindemann ©
All Rights Reserved. Published 2023

Aleph Publications
Manitowoc WI

Paperback Edition
ISBN13: 978-0-9893318-7-6

33 32 31 30 29 28 27 26 25 24   2 3 4 5 6

Dedication

This book is dedicated to everyone who is in a time of trouble or has been toiling in life and feels that they have little to be thankful for, including those who have already been down that path in the past, as well as those who will embark on it in the future. When we are drowning in the rains of life's troubles, it often is difficult to find things to be thankful for. It is my hope and desire that this book gives readers a new perspective allowing everyone to experience Joy and offer gratitude even through those hard times.

Disclaimer

All information, views, thoughts, and opinions expressed herein are those of the author(s) and are being presented only for your consideration and should not be interpreted as advice to take any action. Any action you take with regard to implementing or not implementing the information, views, thoughts, and opinions contained within this published work is your own responsibility. Under no circumstances are distributor(s) and/or publisher(s) and/or author(s) of this work liable for any of your actions.

Anyone, especially those who have been victim of misdirected explanation and understanding, may be best served seeking wise counsel before deciding to implement any information, views, thoughts, opinions, or anything else that is offered for your consideration in this work. All information, views, thoughts, and opinions in this work are not advice, directive, recommendation, counsel, or any other indication for anyone to take any action. All information, views, thoughts, and opinions offered herein are offered only as suggestions for your personal consideration, which is done of your own free will. Your life is your own responsibility; use it wisely.

Any use of trade names or mention of commercial sources is for informational purposes only and does not imply endorsement or affiliation.

Please note that most of the items in quotes in this book are from various versions of the Bible and have been paraphrased.

Contents

Acknowledgements

Usually acknowledgement sections are directed at all of the wonderful people who have assisted an author in life and in the writing and editing process of the book for which the acknowledgements are made. I am now and always will be grateful to and for all of those people.

But this book is different. In this book's acknowledgement section I want to acknowledge the greatness of the Creator, or that which we call "God". It is this Creator that has caused our conscious that allows us to wonder, hope, desire, and create!

It's true that if we had not been born then we would not exist and nothing would matter to us because we would not be here. But we *are* here and most of us don't want to come to an end. It is the Creator who caused our conscious to be, and it is that Creator which we can dwell with and learn from. So Thank You, oh Wondrous Creator for *Being*, for without *You* these words could not exist.

Introduction

There are many things we can say to those around us and to God, but the one thing that we all too often forget to say is, "Thank You". When we do actually manage to remember to thank someone, it's usually done in a lackluster manner with a "yeah, thanks" or just "thanks", and sometimes it's nothing more than a glance of acknowledgement. Is this enough?

Is it enough to offer only a glance of acknowledgement? In some cases, yes, it is enough because when people go overboard with saying "thank you" constantly it can really slow things down and interrupt the flow of life, and we all understand this in our own way. But it's not the muted "thank you" we often offer via a glance of acknowledgement for the little things, it is the lack of thanks for the big things that many, if not most, of us need to address in our own lives.

A proper "*thank you*" can go a long way. I want you to recall how, at some point in your life you likely have done something for someone else. It could have been giving a gift, or simply lending a hand, or helping someone that just got injured, or anything else for which they somehow showed their gratitude and acknowledged you directly by letting you know what a difference your gesture made to them. It's possible that you never experienced this if you're not an outgoing and helpful person, but most people have at some point felt this acknowledgement, and it is quite rewarding.

Some of us are very good at expressing thanks to others, but most of us struggle in that area. Sometimes it's an issue of being shy, and for others it may be an issue of being arrogant and not feeling as if we owe anyone any thanks. But for most of us, it's just a matter of our preoccupation with ourselves, and, more to the point, our preoccupation with our problems.

Life can wind us up pretty tight at times, and as we attempt to mentally process our way out of the tangled web that we have woven, we forget to acknowledge those around us. Nowhere is this more true than with the thanks that we owe to God—our Creator.

People can do some very good things for us and if it's a big enough deal, then we usually find it within ourselves to remember to offer our sincere gratitude and thanks to them, yet we often fail to, or forget to do this with God. Do we owe God any thanks at all? And when life is really beating us up in what appears to be unfair blows, do we have anything to be thankful for? Consider those questions as you read on.

Chapter 1

Realize the Need

Have you ever been down and feeling the weight of the world, and at the same time feeling like you have nothing to be thankful for? Life can hit us pretty hard at times and often it is unfairly so. When we face troubled times in our own lives it's hard to find things for which to be thankful. Even when good friends point out good things that are in our lives, we often still find it hard to be grateful and thankful for those good things. Sure, when things are great it's easy to be thankful, but even then we're usually too busy to give it much thought. The 1954 Irving Berlin song "Count Your Blessings" has a pretty profound statement in it: "When you're worried and can't fall asleep count your blessings instead of sheep."

Being thankful is a peculiar part of us and it has a tendency to shrink or grow depending upon our situation and our attitude. When we're feeling overwhelmed by life and are feeling down we have to work extra hard to coax our thankfulness out of ourselves. Easier said than done, right?

The first part of being thankful is to realize how important it is to others to be acknowledged, which is not easy when life has beaten you down. Yet, if you think about a time when someone recognized *your* good efforts, you then should be able to relate how your acknowledging others makes them feel.

When we offer authentic gratitude to others it has a tendency to grow within us. So, not only does thanking someone make them feel good, but it also makes us feel good when we thank them.

Offering someone something is a gesture, and if that gesture gets rejected it tends to sting—a lot. But when a gesture is accepted, it feels good to us. It doesn't matter if the gesture is us *helping* someone or if it's us *thanking* someone; the general effect on us is the same: It makes us feel good and we want to do it again!

Receiving gratitude when someone thanks you is a powerful motivator for most people. Manipulative people will often offer many thanks because they know that it motivates people to do more. But if our thanks are not sincere, then we will eventually be found out and will most certainly be rejected by those to whom we offer our false-thanks and false-appreciation. Most people have experienced false appreciation. This is not referring to sarcastic "appreciation" that typically occurs when we cause another person to say "gee, thanks" when we do something clumsy like spill our drink on them. Rather we are referring to people who are over-eager with many thank-yous but then they turn around and complain about the gesture they just thanked someone for while sometimes even being mean about it as they share their embellished story with others. It doesn't take long for people to catch on to such lies.

When we think about this scenario we have to try to see things from the Creator's position. Not meaning that the Creator is watching this unfold, but rather in respect to our attitude toward the Creator in giving thanks for *anything* and with any attitude. How do we imagine the Creator feels towards us as we offer our thanks? Are we being authentic? Are we sincere? Does the *thank-you* and our passion or emotion level match up to what we have been given?

Comprehending Our Complacency of Life

It is effort enough for us to try to remember to acknowledge the people who aid us in our lives and do good to us, but with God it's far more difficult for our thanks to match the true value of what we have received from God. Because the pleasures and gifts from the Creator are so vast and so abundant, they are like air to us. We take them in without even noticing any of them.

Our complacency in offering our thanks to God is so bad that we are complacent about our complacency. The problem we have is that these "air opportunities" that we experience every day (as discussed in the book *Understanding Prayer*) is that they have become so common to us that we don't even notice that they exist. We can think of this like a rich kid who happens to be very financially spoiled to a point where they feel entitled to anything they want because they have never been told "No." They just ask and they get it, or expensive things are given to them that they never even have thought to ask for; these things just appear in their life.

We think of such "rich kids" as "spoiled", and by our societal standards they often are. We get frustrated with people like that and we generally don't like it when they behave in an unappreciative manner, typically causing us to want to stay away from them. But their complacency regarding the abundance in their lives is not their fault, it is their parents' fault.

So, is our complacency God's fault? Well... yes and no. Life is life and it deals the hand it deals us in many ways, but some of the abundance that we experience, or don't experience, is our own doing and our own fault. When we place ourselves in advantageous or bad positions, we often thank God or blame God for our circumstances. But very often God has nothing to do with our human choices, because they are **our** *choices.*

To really get a grasp on our complacency regarding the Creator, you have look around you and study your environment. We're not referring to the environment as used in the environmentalism context here; we are looking at the whole of Creation which is far greater. If someone has taken a position that of hating themselves and everything and everyone else, then this won't mean much to them, but when you consider the vast beauty that surrounds all of us and that it's all made voluntarily from nothing, then things start to get pretty interesting.

When you seriously consider how everything came to be, you should be standing in absolute awe at the magnificence of the Created. The essence of Creation is a fairly lengthy and sometimes contentious topic, and to gain a much deeper appreciation, some of the basics of Creation are discussed in the *The Science Of God* book series. When you really think about all of this in a serious way, it's hard to not be awed at Creation. We're talking about the entirety of the "heavens" here, but something as simple as a butterfly is really quite amazing too. Are we then supposed to thank God for **everything**, even oh say... mosquitoes?

We are complacent in our thanks to people, but our complacency towards the Creator and our complacency regarding the thanks we truly owe are truly very overlooked by almost all of us. Try to comprehend your own level of complacency. You will be amazed at just how complacent you likely are.

Our Creative Nature

We each must understand that any information, views, thoughts, and opinions that are offered to us are only for our consideration, and other people who offer us insight are not responsible for the foolish choices we make. It doesn't matter where you get it, even in this book for instance, because *you* are still ultimately responsible for what *you* choose to believe and follow. That's why it's best if you consider various thoughts and weigh the facts to draw your own conclusions. When we fail to process information that is relayed to us and properly put it to use to make great choices, then we fail ourselves. We must all understand that our ability to even consider this is in itself a true gift from God.

Besides the magnificence of all of Creation, we also have to peer into ourselves and into our God-like nature. We are Creative beings, and for this we should be thankful to God. Most of us create and contribute to the world, however, when we fail to contribute then the world becomes a darker place. Cultures that created an environment of withdrawal suffer the consequences of lack of creativity, ultimately ending in destroying themselves and their culture through that lack.

For instance, when communism steals the will of the people by not allowing ownership of effort, it destroys the people's will to create, and without creation any society will eventually fail. There's nothing good that we have that has not been created. Everything that any human has ever made is made from the earth or anything found within it. It is our creating that provides our shelter, our clothing, our food, etc. We could say that someone didn't create the corncob growing in the field, but the work of someone's hand did plant it. And the machinery invented and created by mankind did plant, harvest, and distribute that corn.

We typically think of human creativity as some sort of artistic endeavor, but our creativity is so much broader than only the "arts". Creativity is not only the inventing process, it is also the making process. Any act of making something or assembling something is a part of the creative process. We can use this ability to create only for ourselves, or we can use it create for the betterment of mankind.

We can all make a sandwich for our self and it won't affect the world around us much. It's when we make the sandwich for our fellow man that the world becomes a better place. We're not talking about charity here. Helping with charity is good, but if everyone only took from charity and never gave, then the economy would collapse because eventually we would all be taking and no one would be producing. It's when we do for others that we improve the world and increase it—that's when we create! Most people, when considering this creating topic, will think of "consuming" as being the opposite of creating, and I suppose that's a somewhat fair assessment, but the true opposite of *creation* is *destruction* or theft.

As a simplified view, consider this example: Only you and one other person are stranded on an island, and if the other person made a meal for himself and then you came along and stole his food, you would then eat for a day. You could possibly do this for several days before he would get wise to your nefarious activities, until either he choose to no longer make anything, or he found a way to stop you. And if you somehow were able to always steal his food, thus causing him to never eat, then eventually he would either give up, or die from hunger—and so would you.

It's only when we create and contribute more than we consume, and then share that with others through our wonderful system of commerce that allows the world to be a better place. If we all only take, then nothing would get made or produced or created and we would all be cold, hungry, and eventually dead. We have witnessed this time and time again in countries from all around the world when horrible leaders stole away the will of the people. You would think that the leaders would figure this out after this unfortunate phenomenon has been known for so long and has been seen so often. But, as our foolish human nature would have it, far too many of us humans are blinded by our own greed and covetousness.

It is our creative nature that makes the world a good place to live in. Without it we would all be fighting for space in the same few caves. If our creative nature is not something to thank the Creator for, then nothing is.

Our Concept of God

Who is that old man with the white hair sitting on that big chair? Is it God? No, it's probably Grandpa or old Uncle Joe. God has no body or hands as we do. God doesn't exist in a physical way. Many people have a hard time believing that God exists because God doesn't scientifically *physically* exist, there is no "God detector". But what is "exist" anyway? We'll attack that subject a bit later.

We want to humanize God, so we try to make God into a person. I am not referring to the Christ aspect, but rather the Creative force that through discernment and Creative effort made all things **be** before anything ever was.

When bad things happen we get angry with God and cast our blame on God, saying things like "How could You let this happen to me?" But seldom is God responsible for the stupid things we or others do that have caused our own painful circumstances. If we get cancer, we blame God. And if we are healed, we say "gee thanks" and then forget about the healing we received. We act as if God is some bully torturing us, and when good things come our way we shrug it off as if it's our own great work that saved us, rather than it being the unseen hand of God guiding us.

The Creator is not human, and is not a destroyer, unless it is warranted in order to save creation. The Creator is a Creative Creator who has made everything that we have and everything that we do possible. What will you do with the creative seeds planted within you?

Planting Our Seeds

We've all been given gifts, talents, skills, and passions, and with those seeds we humans accomplish amazing things and commit horrible atrocities. We each get to choose what our seeds will grow for the world. We know all too well the dark side of these seeds, but we're complacent regarding the illuminated side of our seeds. Everyone has the seeds of gifts, talents, skills, and passions within them, but for many people those gifts have been crushed by negativity, causing them to be afraid to allow their seeds to grow because they fear that their treasure of seeds will be trodden under foot again and again by other people's negativity.

What's worse is that many people don't even know that they have these seeds within themselves. Our creative nature is a part of our Creation. It is a natural desire of ours to create, but when we are brought up in an environment of negativity, many of us are never even allowed to discover that those seeds ever existed within us to begin with—and that is a key goal of evil. Yet, the truth is that the seeds always exist in everyone—without fail. It is up to us to come to this realization, each on our own, and then plant and water our seeds to make them thrive so that *we* become an example to others so that *they* too can be creative.

We all need to realize that our creativity can be something as simple as flipping burgers at a local restaurant when our creative nature is being an expert at making delicious burgers. You might not know it and they might not show it, but you are very appreciated by many of your customers when doing so. It is our complacent nature that inhibits us from offering our thanks to those who make our lives more enjoyable because of their doing all of the "simple things" in life.

All people who contribute to the world deserve to be thanked for their contributions, but how much more the Creator who made all things possible?

To Conceive Your Thought

As you move forward in your life while nurturing your own seeds, allow yourself to conceive worthy thoughts, and free your mind from the constraints of "that's impossible" or "I'm not worthy".

Remember, your gift need not be some fantastic world-changing invention. Serving others at a restaurant has equal importance even though it might not touch as many people. You feeding a customer may have kept that person from starving, thus allowing them to offer their own invention to the world. If you have not yet used your true gifts then ask yourself if you ever even knew you had them. But more importantly, consider that you might have been using them all along but didn't realize that those were your gifts.

Do what you do with love, passion, and joy and make the world a better more joyful place for those around you. You could be an attendant at the local gas station and feel like you're not using your gifts. But what if your gift is to make others happy with nothing more than a wonderfully inspiring and friendly disposition that affects people's moods in a positive way for hundreds of weary travelers every day? Everyone has a bad day now and then and something as simple as a kind smile and maybe a bit of small talk can change a person's mood from horrible to great in a matter of seconds. That simple act could save a life by making that person a bit less entrenched in their particular problem. This could make them more aware of their actions allowing them to avoid accidentally running a stoplight and killing another driver or their passengers. You never know what good something as simple as a kind "hello" can do for the world. You must realize that the person who didn't die that day may very well be the child who grows up to be the doctor that saves your grandchild's life.

Conceive your thought and take that thought which comes from your creative God-given spirit, and water it and care for it and allow it to flourish for the good of all mankind. This is the Light that keeps the darkness away.

Trying to Make Things Easy for God

Over the years I have worked with various people and we worked to accomplish the task at hand. And, as is common, when you are designing and building new things that have never existed it can be time-consuming. In attempt to reduce my workload people would make changes to try to make things easier, but this usually resulted in me wasting more time in the long-run and us ending up with something that was less than what it would have been had we not chosen that particular "time-saving" route. I know that I have also done this to others who I hired to do things for me. We do this same thing to God causing ourselves a great deal of delay and frustration. "How so?" you might ask.

We try to make things easy for God by not asking for too much, somehow thinking that the Creator of the entire universe is incapable of producing grand results. Where we get this notion no one really knows, but there is nothing that the Creator has done that is not really quite grand. Even something as insignificant as an insect that we step on and kill without even realizing it is really a very amazing and grand invention.

Through the discouragement of the world and the doubting and disbelief within our own hearts, we don't truly believe that God can produce, so we don't ask. We also run into a problem with our self-worth, believing that we are not worthy to have good things. But either way, we are all in a state of doubt, and *that* is something that God never liked and is directly and indirectly stated throughout the entire Bible.

Doubt is our biggest inhibitor from having the joy we all seek. When we try to tie God's hand with our doubt, we end up doing things like asking for only enough to pay the bills of the day, or that the car makes it through the week. We're always making petty requests because we think it's more possible that those prayers would be answered than something bigger, and therefore we never bother asking for things that are a bit more grand.

Are we really asking for something good when we "just want to get the rent paid this month"? Let's say that God could only allow one good thing in your life per month, what would it be? Would it only be that the car makes it through the month? Or what if God could only do one good thing for you *for your entire life*, then what would you request?

It's a tough balance for us, because if we ask for a lot then we feel as if we are being greedy, which can be true if our heart is in the wrong place. But our requests for good things can also be for reasons that will truly benefit our fellow man.

Let's not inhibit the majesty of God's presence in our lives by asking for petty meaningless things. Let's ask God for resources that will advance and enlighten ourselves along with the rest of world. When we only focus on the little patches in life, it's much like when people tried to save me time or I tried to save them time by trying to make things "easier", only to cause more work in the long run and end up with a somewhat inferior end product. When this route is chosen, the person for whom the work is being done suffers the consequences. The same is true in our own lives, except in our own lives the work is being done *for* us. *We cause ourselves* many delays in life, because, in our complacency, we don't realize the true majesty and Creative nature of the Creator. And in doing so we cause our concept of God to be incompetent and lackluster, as opposed to conceiving what is really true about God.

Plant and nurture the seeds of your gifts, and don't try to shove the Creator of the Universe into your own tiny mental box of doubt. Take some time to look to the heavens and at the intricacy of nature and then give thanks to God for all things and for your ability to realize and understand and create. Believe that good things can be done in your life—things that are beyond your willingness to believe.

Chapter 2

Happy to Exist

What really does it mean for something to "exist"? Do you *exist*? The subject of existence can quickly get rather philosophical and end in meaningless petty debate, but we're going to be a bit more practical here. The first point to consider is what *existence* actually is. If you're holding something in your hand then it exists. This is made evident by the fact that you can see it and feel it in your hand. But what about you? Do *you* really exist? Of course you do, and that fact is made evident by simply looking at your hands and clapping them together to hear the sound and then clasping or rubbing your hands together to feel them. But is that really actually *you* that you're feeling or seeing? This is the point where things get cloudy for us and where philosophical and scientific debate enters the discussion.

"Scientifically" and in a godless sense, we think that our body is us, and when the body dies then that is our end. But this is greatly debated and is highly doubtful, and it is where people choose different schools of thought. Yet it doesn't matter what we choose because there is a truth and that truth will stand no matter what *we* choose to believe. So if the truth is that we *only* exist while our body lives and breathes, but we think that we will have an afterlife in Heaven, then we will be wrong. Or if the truth is that there's an afterlife and we choose to think that we end when our body ends, then we will be wrong.

We get to choose what we believe about our existence, but we don't get to choose if that existence ends at our death or if our soul lives on, or if there will be an actual bodily resurrection. The reason that many people don't believe in existence beyond the last breath is because anything beyond the last breath is not scientifically evident at this point in our cumulative human scientific research.

So the question I ask to those who are not sure if we have a soul that exists beyond our body is this: Since the body still exists even after it's dead, then whose body is it? Right now if you hurt your hand and I ask you what happened, you would likely say "I cut my hand." "<u>My</u> hand" states ownership, just as does the term "my body". So *who* is possessing your "my body"?

Our existence is more than just our physical body vessel, which will be discussed later. We are beings of *conscious*, and that *conscious* is a truly amazing phenomenon. We can try to discredit other-life existence and demand that "souls" are not real, but that won't change things if the truth is otherwise.

The truly interesting part about our existence is that many of us fear death. Some people say that they fear possible suffering leading up to death, but many people, if not most people, who fear death, fear what will happen to them *after* death. This is why so many people try to deny that an afterlife or other-life exists. But, such denials won't change whatever is actually true.

So the question comes down to this: Does our *conscious* continue outside of the body after the body is dead? There's much testimony that there is an "other-life" aspect to all of us. I refer to it as "other-life" because if we are still alive and if we are not actually our body but are instead *in* our body, then "afterlife" is not an appropriate term whether or not our body still has the breath of life in it.

Where does our joy come from? Do the chemicals of the body create joy? No, the chemicals do not create joy. Our good and healthy body chemistry is a *result* of joy. When we feel joy, we feel it because we are in a good state and our mind is content and is in a state of pure pleasure. This joyful state of conscious affects the chemistry that the body produces because we are happy to simply exist in this state.

Our Womb In Space

There are two states of existence, one being the physical tangible realm, and the other being the realm of conscious. But does our conscious have to live somewhere? We can address that another time, but our physical body does have to live somewhere.

When you don't believe that a discerning Creator exists then you are at a very great disadvantage in life. This is because you're then unable to realize important connections and analogical aspects that give hints at why something is as it is or what it means. Let's use the womb of a woman as an example. A womb is an empty place where a child is conceived and is created, which is much like our womb in space or the atmosphere of our Earth on which we all live. The membrane of our water-laden atmosphere allows us to breathe and surrounds us and protects us as we grow as a human race. Without this womb we would all be dead within a minute's time.

It's interesting to listen to people who want to inhabit Mars when they believe we are going to destroy the Earth and that Mars would be more habitable. We could set off all of the nuclear bombs and release all of the pollutants at one time and our Earth is still going to be thousands of times more "habitable" than are Mars or the Moon. I don't mean to discourage exploration of other planets or heavenly bodies, but to think that somehow we can live there like we do here on Earth is a nonsensical perspective. We may someday have remote stations on the Moon or Mars where people can live, and we may actually be able to take resources from those places. But nothing we do to them or Earth is likely to ever make them *more* habitable than Earth is now or ever will be no matter what we do to Earth or Mars or any other planets or moons.

Earth is unique in our solar system as it circles the Sun. It's a wonderful womb-like planet that nourishes us and allows our bodies to exist. Without the Earth none of us would be here because our bodies would not be here to allow our conscious to grow and learn. The breath of life was breathed into Adam and has been passed down from woman to child ever since. The air that we breathe is nothing more than air, but the *fact* that we breathe is what is truly amazing. Just as a mother breathes for her child when her blood oxygen is delivered to the child through the placenta which is temporarily attached to the womb, so too are we able to breathe from the womb of Earth. Should we not be thankful to God for this too?

Existing In All that Surrounds You

Why do we exist anyway? Our existence is dependent upon actually having been born or conceived. Once our conscious has been created *we are* and we exist along with our body until our body dies, then our existence or conscious carries on. While we live and breathe on Earth, we exist in all of the wonders that surround us. Look around you and see all that exists.

We can look at the heavens or nature or even, using science, at the smaller parts of physical existence and marvel at the consistency of unique patterns. Interesting isn't it, the term "unique pattern"? In our human way we create patterns to make things identical, yet in nature we see pattern all over but the items are not "identical". Leaves, snowflakes, and even us humans all follow pattern in our Creation, yet we are all very different. People say that no two snowflakes are identical and no two finger prints are identical and yet we recognize them as snowflakes or as finger prints, or maple leaves as *maple* leaves.

We see vast beauty all around us and all of it allows our bodies to exist while giving us much joy. There are few if any adults who by the time of their death will not at some point in life have found joy in the vast beauty that surrounds us.

We exist in all that surrounds us, but do we take the time to take it in and thank the Creator for it? Probably not as much as we should because we get so wrapped up in our own self-imposed day-to-day problems that we miss the beauty surrounding us all. We all need to take more time to appreciate the Creation that surrounds us. Some people wrongly go so far as to offer a sort of worship of nature and in doing so they miss God entirely.

If you're a parent you have probably given your child a gift and took great joy in watching them as they experience the joy of your gift even if they failed to thank you for it. It is seeing the joy that we can bring to others that brings our own true joy. When we take joy in and notice Creation and exist in all that surrounds us, it gives the Creator great pleasure. Thanking the Creator for all of it will offer even greater joy for both us and for the Creator.

Our Existence Fills a Place

On the two levels of existence, the *physical* and the *non-physical*, we have our spirit, or soul, in our body, and then our body in the world. Our bodies are Created to be filled with our conscious and that conscious is made whole as we sense the world around our body *with* our body. Loneliness is a horrible thing for us humans. We like to have peace and quiet once in a while, but to forever be alone with no contact with other living beings would be a horribly lonely existence.

Imagine the Creator before any Creation took place. For, to us, what is probably billions or even trillions of years, the Creator may have had conscious and no one to share with until Creatures were Created. But animals and other creatures don't have the same nature as man. If you're a parent, then ask yourself why you chose to have children. Was it for the trouble children can cause? No, it was likely because you wanted to create a child like you that you can love and care for, which is why we get so protective when someone tries to lead our children astray. The world that we live in, along with our lives and bodies, are all models of the God-to-man relationship– **We** are God's children.

We fill a place in the heart of the Creator and are made in the Image of that Creator. We typically think of this in the physical form of our body being "Created in the image of", and it is, but not as a duplicate of some physical God. Rather, our having been "Created in the image of" is more regarding our God-like nature. The Creator wanted companionship with beings like the Creator. We humans fill a void in the heart of the Creator in the same way that our children fill a void in our own hearts—Our existence fills a place in the heart of the Creator.

The People Who Exist Around Us

Our existence fills more than the void in God's heart, our existence also fills the void in other people's hearts and their existence fills a place in our own. The people who exist around us came into conscious the same way that we ourselves did, through conception, birth, and growing. Our conscious, or our soul, wouldn't **_be_** without that experience—it simply would not exist.

It's amazing that we can communicate with those around us using words or sounds and actions. Just consider the simple complexity of words; words are assembled sounds that we can also represent using symbols or letters and then share that with others. We can share words in printed or verbal form so that the receivers of those words can interpret them and respond back to us in a dialog that can have infinite variations of meanings.

To exist and converse with the people who surround us is truly something to be thankful for. To convey a thought to another consciousness is the most amazing of all of the gifts that we have ever been given. We can ponder something and come to conclusions and discuss those theories with others, and then they can then also embark on the same line of thought and share their thoughts with us.

If you're a person who talks to and listens to God when you pray, then you probably have a good grasp on this amazing ability to communicate our thoughts to God, or to our fellow man through speech. When you're in prayer or communication with the Creator, make sure to offer a great deal of thanks and praise for all of the people around you who have taught you good things and who you can offer your love to and receive love from, all while you communicate with them soul to soul and spirit to spirit.

We Exist Outside of Time

Time is an interesting feature of our existence, but we often misunderstand *time*. Time is discussed in the books *Bending The Ruler* and a bit in the *The Science Of God volumes*, but time is not really what we think it is. Some people believe that we can travel through time if only we could travel fast enough, but that's not likely to happen. We humans have a tendency to misunderstand much about science and physics.

Time is a measurement of the existence of something. If you read Genesis chapter one very carefully, as is done in the *The Science of God Volumes,* you'll see that the "great lights" were made to be "for signs and for seasons and for days and years". Those are all terms of measurement of something. God basically made a giant clock that measures existence, not *how much* we exist but rather *how long* we exist. But our spirit—the true essence of us—truly exists outside of time as measured.

We don't need the clock to exist. And the counting of time, while handy, is of little use to our actual existence. Though regarding our salvation, markers of time are important because at some point we can watch the giant clock and realize that our time is drawing near, and while we remain in our body we still have the opportunity to repent and obtain salvation. But once that time has expired, it appears that our opportunity to follow Truth also expires when we have not chosen to do so before death.

Because we exist outside of the physical and outside of time we are certain to live on, and if we have chosen a path of lies rather than a path of Truth, then we still have to live on, but we must then live with our lies, thus forcing the Truth to be far from us.

We typically think of existing in our lies as punishment from God, but I'm not so sure about that. It's possible and highly likely that it's more of a technical function of not being in Truth. If you choose to believe lies, then you are stuck in those lies until you follow a different path and find Truth. But we might not be able to do that after we lose our physical body because our conscious might be eternally caught in the falsehoods and darkness that we chose during our physical life.

It is our ability to follow Truth that we need to work to perfect, and then we also need to actually *follow* Truth to make sure that we don't end up in eternal darkness unable to alter our thinking and our chosen path. Our salvation is a gift of monumental proportions and we must thank God every day for that gift. The problems we face on Earth are short and usually end in a relatively short time of days, weeks, or months. But *eternal* is on an entirely different plane, and when we reach that plane we certainly want to be seeing the Light.

Thank God the Creator for our salvation so that as we exist outside of time we can exist in the Light of and with the Creator, rather than being trapped in eternal darkness.

Chapter 3

Rise Up When Times Get Tough

When we struggle during our tough times we need to have something, or some thought, to grab hold of to help to pull us through. This is why God is so important for so many of us. We live in a society that sees struggle as "failure", rather than as the opportunity for extensive learning that it is. Sure it hurts during the painful struggle-education period, but when we choose to utilize that time and the lessons learned as guides to our future, it then becomes invaluable to us. It's during our struggle-education process that being close to God is often quite helpful and strengthens us, thus allowing us to rise up when times get tough while helping us endure the pain of those times.

It's not particularly comforting hearing these things as we suffer through those times because we typically already know this, yet most people's "tough times" don't really compare to something such as the suffering of being beaten and then nailed to a cross.

Rise up and stand strong when times get tough because those times are a test of your real value, and your personal future worth and life is determined by your choices during those times–every day is a new chance to get it right. When we're weak and panic we then lose our advantage by making bad choices, only serving to extend our tough times. Stand tall and be strong and give thanks to God in all you do and in all you experience. We need not thank God for the torturous pain, however we can and should thank God for our ability to conceive our way out and learn from those tough experiences. This ability and skill is invaluable and worthy of much gratitude to God for it.

The Tougher It Gets the Tougher It Gets

Why is it that when we're down the kicks of life tend to get harder and harder? Who needs such cruelty and unfairness?

It doesn't matter that life is unfair because the unfairness is coming whether we like it or not. It is each our own our task to rise up and learn how to deal with *and defeat* the unfairness.

The problem that many of us run into when times get tough is that, as mentioned earlier, we panic and make poor choices only serving to make matters worse for ourselves. It's bad enough that life is unfair and kicks us when we're down and that the world around us doesn't seem to care, but what we don't need is to kick ourselves when we're down. When things get tough we need to **take care to <u>not</u> do the wrong things**–things that only serve to increase the length of time that we will struggle and intensify the problems we struggle with.

It is our ability to rise up and stand strong in the face of this unfairness that allows our escape from those bonds of darkness. This is true whether or not life is fair, and it is so regardless of how tough life becomes. The more we are willing to stand strong and endure, then the more we learn and can guide our future. Understanding this makes us question: How exactly do we rise up and stand strong?

The High Ground During Rains of Trouble

We all know that life kicks us at times, but when our soul dwells in the right place then we can avoid the deluge of frustration we typically experience when tough times do rain down upon us. The high ground for us can be good friends or good family or even any person who inspires us. Certainly we should seek the higher ground when troubles occur, but if we choose to seek high ground only amongst friends or family or other positive inspiration then we must be ready to tread water on our own, because people, even great ones, can let us down when we need them the most.

Anyone who has ever gotten beaten up by life's cruel blows is probably familiar with being let down regarding hoped-for support during tough times. I'm not talking about someone lending us money or actually helping us work or anything else along those lines. I'm referring to support of the spirit. When we look to *man* as our foundation then that foundation is only as strong as the strongest person's faith and ability to offer their support to us. But as life would have it, when troubles rain down we often find that the others can't swim well either. And sometimes we end up trying to tread water as they panic and cause us to have to work all the harder to stay afloat while keeping them afloat too.

I understand that this sounds terribly discouraging, but if we depend *only* on other humans then the odds run very high that we will be disappointed when their support is lacking or altogether gone. However, if you happen to have really great people surrounding you, then it's typically better. But when we are solely dependent on them to keep our spirits high during tough times, we then have an increased risk of being inadvertently let down by them so much more than if we select the proper ground and foundation to set our hope upon.

The most critical reason to not depend upon others is that they likely have families and problems of their own, and if they are typical humans then their own lives will come before ours. In general, other people owe us nothing, and their support for our goals and their love of us not really their concern when we face trouble. We must consider anything good we get from them as a gift and not as something we are deserving of. Their voluntary love for us is their option, as is ours towards them. With regard to mankind, our best high ground is our self, but our ultimate high ground is God.

Mankind's Place is Higher than We Imagine

There are far too many of us that feel devalued and unworthy. These feelings about ourselves are no help to us when things get tough and the heavy rains of trouble and depression begin. But there is no time more important to realize our place in Creation than when we are in very rough waters. What is "our place in Creation"?

According to Genesis chapter one, mankind was the last Created in the account of Creation. The heavens and the plants and the other creatures came first, and then after everything was prepared, mankind was made and then placed in the "Garden" to keep it. There is no other mention of any other tangible creature having such a unique role in the care of anything spoken of in the Bible. Our in-the-image-of-God-like qualities put us in a unique position relative to the rest of Creation—We were put there to tend it.

Imagine what life would be like if some extremely wealthy person came to you and said "I need to care for my home, but I am never there and I need it maintained. You can live there for free, indefinitely, as long as you abide by two simple rules. The first rule is to care for it and the second rule is, don't eat any fruit from the tree in the back yard."

I think that most people would be very pleased with such an arrangement because the entire place would be taken care of at your own discretion. All of your needs would be met in that agreement and you could basically live there for free forever. Every need you have would be included. Such a deal would be a very good deal with only the two simple conditions already mentioned.

The rich man would be placing a great deal of trust in you by making such an offer, showing that he believes that *you are worthy*. This is the same deal that Adam and Eve had, but they unwisely chose to defy that agreement and were tossed out into the cold. Yet even though they violated the agreement, they were still given an opportunity to return at some point if they would prove worthy and accept a very generous offer.

In our example, the generous offering is made by the rich man's son and he will take the penalty for your violations in order to make things right for you. Both the rich man and his son would have to hold you in very high regard if they were willing to forgive your foolish error by allowing the rich man's son to pay for it.

The fact that we are held in such high regard by both The Creator and The Christ is truly a sign unto us that we have immense value to them and to Creation. But we must all stop falling short as a habit and instead work towards building our foundation on high ground.

Building Our Foundation On High Ground

Using friends, family, and others as high ground can work, but if they are intended to be our foundation, then they will likely be washed away when life's troubles rain down upon us. Our true high ground is that higher Light that leads our way. It is Truth that will protect us when tough times come.

We often have the thought that if we just stand by God we will be protected from all bad things. But this is not said anywhere in the Bible. Some could argue that the Israelites were protected while wandering in the desert, and this is true, but they were not protected from their own stupidity and foolish mistakes. They all still had to deal with each other and each other's errors. What they were protected from was the disease and starvation that the cities around them endured, most of which were results of bad and foolish behavior. The Israelites were not given a pass to anything; they were given the instructions for good health and joyous lives.

There is nowhere in the Bible that says that we will be unconditionally protected in this world. Not even Adam and Eve were completely protected in the Garden of Eden. They had two vulnerabilities: Those vulnerabilities were the Tree of the Knowledge of Good and Evil, and the Serpent. And just as the Israelites violated their good deal, so too did Adam and Eve. If we think we are any different, then guess again. We are all just as bad or even worse, yet we are still are all truly valued by God.

We must set our foundation upon the high ground of the Light of Truth and we will all be a lot better off for doing so. When we raise ourselves up just a little bit by making the right choices we then will be raised up higher by the Light of Truth and by the Creator who values us more than we ourselves do.

Just consider how we value humans if you doubt we have a low opinion of ourselves as a culture overall. Many people put animals before humans. It's not wrong to hold animals in high regard and we should be kind to animals, but should we not be even more kind to our fellow man? Consider the efforts towards implementing laws making it a felony to be cruel to animals. Oddly, the organizations supporting such legislation kill more animals than anyone. Now compare the idea of making it a felony to be cruel to an animal versus the idea of murdering a preborn human baby. If these efforts and actions don't show us that we have devalued our true worth to a point that we have placed ourselves below even animals, then we can expect that our next collective error will be to devalue ourselves even below trees and other plants. This must never happen!

Our high ground is the Creator and the Light of Truth of that Creator. Deliberately forcing ourselves into a lower position is similar to when Adam and Eve followed the advice of the Serpent and took and ate of the Tree of The Knowledge of Good and Evil.

Let us all get this point clearly defined in our heads and realize that *we are special*. Not necessarily entitled, but special. We have been Created above the animals and plants and we are worthy of salvation for our foolish human errors when, and only when, we choose to seek the high ground of the Glorious Light Of Truth.

It is important that we all realize the gift that the high ground of the Light of Truth is. If we fail to come upon this realization then we are certain to not be thankful for it. Of all of the things to be grateful to God for, this Light is certainly at the top of the list right next to Creation itself.

When we do not understand this Light, then our good judgement is typically severely impaired. This is why so many of us have so many troubles raining down upon us causing us to run to people for hope of refuge for any relief we can find.

There are many people who have this Light, but that number is far too low. This is the Light that people seek when they try to be "enlightened". But often what they find on their enlightenment journey is trivial knowledge that, without the wisdom that Truth brings, is often of more harm to us than it is good.

Take refuge in the Light of Truth and you will need no other high ground to stand upon when trouble comes your way. Often when we suffer troubles, only time and wise choices can solve those problems for us. But when we are on True high ground, then it is far easier to endure those troubles, and for this we owe a great deal of gratitude to God.

Life is Not Always Fair

If you think you are doing your best in life you had better stop and actually ask yourself if you truly are doing *your* "best", especially when life seems unfair. We can do our daily work and still get pummeled by life, making life seem very unfair to us. But in truth, the "unfair" things that occur in our lives are often due to our own complacency and lack of willingness to *really* do our best. So sometimes we somewhat deserve those tough times, because in essence we are just being lazy.

But for those who are truly giving their all and working hard towards their good goals, life is still not always fair. Our world is full of contaminations that we all have created ranging from intangible toxic attitudes all the way down to tangible toxins in our food. If you're one who has not contributed to the more toxic aspects of life, you may still be the subject of the toxins' target, whether it's a toxic spirit of someone coming at you, or if you're being affected by toxic chemicals in your daily life. Unfairness often comes at us harder the more innocent we are and the more grand our goals are in utilizing our gift-seeds spoken of earlier.

It is our ability to rise up and stand against and bear these troubles, trusting that God will guide us through those toxic troubled times—Did you get that?—**Guide** us through. Let **us** not be someone else's toxin, but instead let us be their nutrition full of inspiration and direction that they may follow our example of perseverance, so that they too can rise up out of the murky fires of dark times.

When we're lazy and bad things happen to us, life seems unfair, but in such cases it is often either very fair or unfair in that we are not really getting what we truly deserve. Sometimes we ought to be punished to match our foolishness, but are not. We typically only get a light slap on the hands, where on the other hand those who actually deserve reward sometimes get the unfair exchange that life often dishes out.

We can add to all of this that we now have created a culture where *stupid* is rewarded and decency is penalized. In our high-tech world we have created good technology, but we use it unwisely by appealing to the darker desires of humanity, all for the sake of riches. A good person might make a minor comment that is not "liked" by someone else and the "someone else" will comment back and then exchange it with other like-minded people who then make it their mission to destroy someone for some petty comment that is often nothing more than a funny little quip about some current event or maybe some foolhardy thing they said many years ago. It certainly is not fair that we would collectively destroy the life of a person who made a minor comment in poor judgement in the eyes of others.

Also, consider the flip-side of our high-tech world and look at the cruelty and graphic imagery that is making people rich for offering nothing at all constructive to the world. All this is occurring while many hard-working people who create everything we enjoy that actually assists us in life might suffer in near poverty.

Life is seldom "fair", and it is our job to overcome this unfairness and conquer it. You can and will conquer when you embrace Truth. We must rise up and lead others in giving thanks and appreciation to God for our strength and for our ability to do so. Doing this will inspire us ourselves *and* those around us.

Chapter 4

We All Must Seek the Way

The Light of Truth is the high ground that we all desire, but our problem is that we can't seem to find our way there. There is a straight path to get there, but we are all generally too blind to see it. Sometimes we find what appears to be a good guide to lead our way, but we soon find that we and our guide have gone terribly off course and we have gotten lost. When our way is lighted by the Light of Truth, then finding our way becomes far easier.

This is where and why we struggle so much. Sure, when we have the Light it's easier to find our way, but we have to actually look for the path to begin with. And in order to actually look for the path we first have to realize that the path exists.

This is one of those if-you-don't-know-then-I-am-not-going-to-tell-you type situations. We all need to come to the realization that paths do exist and that there is a path to the Light and a path to our destination. When we don't know or understand this then we won't even know to look for those paths. If we don't know enough to look, then we're in a bit of trouble because when we don't look it is very difficult to even come upon the notion that *any* paths exist, let alone our own actual personal paths.

But here is another problem that we face: There are people begging us to pay attention, some even practically screaming for us to take notice of this Light and the paths leading to it and to our personal destinations. Yet we say "I'm not interested" or "I don't believe in that stuff".

Making Your Own Path

Depending upon what we are discussing, there are many paths, but the path to salvation is straight and there is only one. Yet for our earthly problems there can be many paths leading to our destination, plus we can have more than one destination, and for this too we must show our appreciation.

We're very narrow-minded and have a one-track mind, meaning that we get a vision in our head and we decide that the path we see in our mind is the *only* path to our chosen destination, but it is not. There are many ways we can achieve our goals, and we each need to make our own path to those goals. Consulting with others is sometimes a good idea so that we're being challenged; thus forcing us to prove our ideas to be true and good, but our path is no one else's responsibility but our own. If we can find some assistance then that's okay and good, but in the end it's our own path and only we are responsible for finding it. Troubles in our lives or no troubles, our path must be made by us alone. When we allow others, or even force others, to forge our path for us, then it is not our path and we have no one to blame but ourselves when things don't turn out the way we had hoped, as is all too common.

Finding the Right Path

Making a path is different than finding your best one. While we can have many paths to our desired outcome, there are usually only a couple, or even only one, that makes the most sense and will be the most expedient for us and give us the best return for our efforts.

When we seek a path for our desires, many of us fail to ask if our desire is truly *our own* desire or if it is someone else's desire. Many of us have no specific burning desire to do anything, but will try to fulfill our lack of desire by copying others. This isn't bad, but it also is not necessarily good that we're lukewarm. It is when we have passion for something good that we do our best work and bring the most value to ourselves, to the world, and, most importantly, to the Creator.

There's a certain risk to people when they hear, or are told, to release their inhibitions because often this is interpreted by them as a need to do something that is opposed to what is good for them and/or for the world. But the notion of releasing our inhibitions has nothing to do with rebellion or doing unwise things that cause you to have to live with the consequences for the rest of your life; nor is releasing our inhibitions doing things that may live on in society damaging scores of our fellow man long afterwards.

There's a price to be paid by us for the harm that we cause others and ourselves when we follow wrong paths. We will not be shorted on punishments for our foolish choices. "Releasing your inhibition" is *not* rebellion. It means to not withhold your true self and your *good* ideas because of fear of what other people might say. Nearly all of the most common and best inventions, which also happen to be the most revolutionary, were often mocked and the inventors were thought of as "eccentric" by their neighbors and other people who worked in the same or similar industries. Some of these inventors were even negatively cast in media with stories that carried a tone of mockery about them.

But people who do great things look ahead and see the benefits and rewards of their ideas and they are willing to suffer the interim consequences of their passion. The excitement and passion that they feel and have towards their work overrides the doubting and mockery of their foolish non-believing counterparts. Those people who didn't believe in the ideas of the inventors and mocked them for their efforts, always end up being users or customers of the invention and of the inventor.

When we're able to find that which builds and increases the world and society at large, and we are passionate about doing it, then that may very well be our best or right path. But we must realize that our personal path is not necessarily us inventing some revolutionary device or method. It can be as simple as being that joyous face that greets hundreds of people a day at the local gas station. It's surprising how few of us understand this and how long it took those who do realize this to actually realize it.

Find your personal path because it is the right path for you, and know that if that path doesn't increase and improve the world and those all around you, then it's likely not the right path for you or anyone else.

Opportunity Abounds On Your Personal Path

As you follow your path, that path should bring you much joy. You will find opportunity abounds when you are on that path. But understand that some destinations are shorter-term and generally have quicker payback and are not as impactful as the great invention someone else might have spent a lifetime creating. So the person with the joyous smile that greets us at the gas station will feel much of their reward for their passion immediately, where a person who is creating something brand new will typically have to plow through much negativity and endure it until they have proven their invention worthy in the eyes of their fellow man—only then do their big rewards come; though the journey itself is also a reward for those ingenious people.

There is no perfect general life path, there are only perfect individual paths, and the "right path" for you is going to be one that brings you and others the most joy and is in accordance with God. When we share our gifts while we are brimming with joy and Truth, then opportunity is close at hand. People are more interested in us and our lives when they can feel the joy we have within us. When people notice our joy it often makes others curious causing them to ask us questions. This can lead to lots of opportunity when the right people cross our paths.

If we stay sheltered and secluded and never allow our passion and joy to be seen, then it is unlikely that we will succeed in bringing it to the world. What many of us don't realize is that the person or people who can help us are generally tuned in to the key signs of what they and we do, or they are tuned in to the people that they know who have connections to help us advance in life and in our efforts. So if you share what you do with your gifts, either through serving other people or telling them about what you do, then those people who are tuned in to those ideas will recognize those gifts in you. And if your ideas are worthy, then those people are likely to help you or help to spread the word about you to the proper people.

Get yourself on to *your* right path because when those people cross your path that's when great things happen for many of us. Even that joyous smile can bring opportunity for those who are true to their self as they greet their customers. We seek out passionate people and when we see passion we tend to have a desire to see that passion being put to good and even great use.

When You Have Found the Way

When you have found your path and the way has been made clear, you can quickly gain a great deal of momentum. It is difficult for others to stop this kind of momentum. The world is full of competition with people trying to be above everyone else, but when we do good things with passion and joy, it's a joy for the Creator because that is what we have been created for.

Imagine the Creator being conscious and alone pondering for trillions of years and at some point realizing that the vast empty darkness could be raised to a new level with a way or method just by speaking it and pulling things together by Creating and then separating to make things such as stars and planets. Also imagine working to keep it in place as the gravity, which is the result of the Created, receives the nearby elements and these many tiny pieces come together. Then through the guide of gravity, movement begins as if it is a living thing. The Creator must have been amazed and filled with great joy as this all occurred. As the bodies in the heavens move around each other they support each other. And while they are all the same in that they are giant orbs of matter, they are all uniquely different. As we see these stars, planets, and moons they speak for the desire and passion of the Creator as they represent the Creator but are not the Creator. The bodies of the heavens are separate from the Creator and they cause us to question why and how, allowing us to be able to discern and make the choice to believe in eternal Truth. The passion of the Creator is probably beyond our comprehension because the Creation of the heavens is amazing, and the Creation of souls is even more astounding. If we are passionate about our human achievements that are all only done through the master achievements of the Creator, then just think of the Creator's level of passion for us.

When you have found your path, you're likely to feel great joy as your good passion is being fulfilled while you venture down your good path. It is the *journey* down the path to our destination that brings much of our joy, along with the ultimate destination itself.

Whatever You Ask In My Name and Do Not Doubt

Doubt is a tool that is easy to abuse, and our doubt is a destroyer of us. The Christ said "Whatever you ask in my name and do not doubt will be given to you." But most of us do not know this because most of us have never read the Bible. The Bible is a very interesting tool that people spend their lives studying, and yet we can still miss some very good points in it.

There are far too many people that wrongly believe that "the Bible is just a bunch of stories", but that is perhaps the most ignorant thing anyone could ever say or think. It takes only a very small amount of research to realize that the Bible is a set of books that are written accounts of history of a line of people leading to the Christ, along with some brief history that occurred after the Christ.

But because of the errors in translations of some Bible versions that came after the printing revolution of the 1800's, people began to have erred interpretations and erred understanding of what the Bible truly says. For instance, in the *The Science of God* book series it discusses how Genesis chapter one is misunderstood by many people because of recent erred translations of the Bible. Then, because the very foundation of the Bible is clouded with errors, the people to whom these translation problems are *not* known believe wrongly and misunderstand what Genesis chapter one is actually saying; then when we get challenged and subsequently humiliated about our erred beliefs regarding the Creation account, we turn away from God because of our ignorance and humiliation. When we find ourselves without explanation due to our erred understanding, we lose faith. Then the *doubt* that us humans have such an affinity for becomes ever greater in our hearts.

"And do not doubt" is quite a feat for us humans, and we just can't seem to get around this. We have been given many promises from God and yet we doubt them all. But when some arrogant college professor or some arm-chair-know-it-all comes along and tells us the Bible is just stories or a bunch of lies, then we foolishly believe them.

"Whatever you ask for in My name and do not doubt will be given unto you" is a very big promise, and yet most of us cannot find it in ourselves to receive this promise, let alone even believe it, or in most cases even have read it or know that it exists.

But let us understand also that the "*whatever*" part of this promise must be good and not harm innocent people. It must build up and create, rather than tear down and destroy. The Creator is one who Creates good, and will even be reluctant to destroy evil because evil could change and choose to do good at some point and therefore no longer be evil. So for us to imagine that we somehow could ask for something that is not good and have it given unto us is a foolish notion. "Asking in My name" carries with it the obvious sentiment that what you ask must be good for all of mankind. It doesn't necessarily have to affect *all* of mankind; it just needs to not harm that which is good.

So we could *believe* but not *receive* because what we are asking for does not create or build up. Additionally, it is possible that sometimes we get what we asked for but it fails for us because, as discussed in the book *Understanding Prayer*, what we ask for will always have some consequences, and sometimes those consequences are not in themselves bad, but we don't like them because we hang on too tightly to *our own view* of the way we think things ought to be.

When we "ask in My name" we very well may be "given unto" but when we hang on too tightly to the old, then the great new things that the Creator prepares for us are often overlooked or outright rejected by us because we can't see them due to our doubt and our focus on the old which bars us from receiving the new. We all need to shut up and listen after we ask in thanks-giving.

We owe God and the Christ a great deal of thanks for the "whatever you ask for in My name" promise alone—even if our own faith is too weak to achieve it. Strengthen your faith and ask for good things and do not doubt, and then give Glory and Praise to the Most High God, The Creator.

Chapter 5

A Breath of Fresh Air

When we conceive our ideas and realize that our *paths* actually exist, then we can rise up and stand strong and find our own path that leads the way to our own blessed future. It is this fundamental ability that allows all that we do. For this ability alone we owe a great debt of gratitude to the most high God during both good *and* bad times. Without this ability nothing much would ever change and we would not have the ability to change the course of our own future.

A Whisper of Your Breath

While it is good to sometimes shout from the mountain tops and proclaim the Glory of God, the Creator is generally very quiet. And we have no need to shout when praying or talking to God. But with our inability to have strength of faith and our inability to see things clearly, and quickly understand them, we need to say things out loud so that *we ourselves* hear them.

It's odd but true that we can think things in our mind and that they might not register in our head until we actually say those things out loud. When we talk to the Creator we can think the discussion in our mind, but there's great value to us in speaking it in a whisper—actually saying it in a physical way. Again, we don't need to shout from the mountain tops, though we can, but the whisper of your breath has great value when praying to God. It is when we verbalize it physically with our breath that we ourselves can become more aware and solidify our thoughts in our own mind.

Just as our body helps our conscious to *become*, so too our verbalizing in a whisper-volume helps the thoughts of our conscious become evident to ourselves.

We can hear or read something a thousand times over and not grasp the underlying or intended message. We can think about it for years and miss it entirely, but when we begin to *ask* these things with the breath of our existence, it is then that clarity can more easily come to us. The Christ said "whatever you ask for in My name", but if we don't speak it then did we really ask?

Of course our communication with the Creator is on another level, but if you ask something of a friend and you do it only in your mind, then don't be angry with your friend if they never do it because they probably didn't hear your thoughts. Our thoughts are powerful and important, and those thoughts are expressed through voice. Use your voice and offer the whisper of your breath to ask of and to glorify the Creator.

The Spirit of Things

When we think of "spirit", we often think of "team-spirit" or attitude towards something. Our *emotions* are really what are being referred to in this case and they are very important when praying. This is all explained in the book *Understanding Prayer*, and it matters a great deal when we talk to the Creator. If we fail to speak with passion in our heart then our speech is lackluster and it has little power, but when we speak with true passion and really show our authentic team-type spirit about our desire, it has a lot more meaning to us and to God.

To get a good visual picture of this idea, consider electricity. Most of us have either used or we have a light dimmer switch somewhere in our home, or at least on our vehicle's dashboard lights. Think of your passion as the amount of power that is allowed to flow to the lights after if passes through the dimming switch. When we have the lights dimmed it can be very hard to have a clear view as we look around, but when we turn the dimmer up to full power the light can be rather bright, making it very easy to see everything in the room.

There are times when it is good to have dimmed passion, but when we're asking anything of the Creator our passion should be true and not subdued. You might look at this as you must have a great amount of excitement, but while that is okay, that in itself is not passion. For instance, you could be in a situation that is causing you much difficulty and pain in one aspect of your life where you might be experiencing a great amount of sorrow. This sort of passion is usually very quiet but is no less passionate than when we are very excited about something.

Passion has nothing to do with volume of voice or being visually happy. Passion cannot be faked because passion is in your heart. Throughout your life you will likely recall others or maybe even yourself being expressive on the outside but hurting on the inside. You or they may have outwardly shown a great amount of excitement, but internally were in great torment. During those times, the true passion is not outwardly shown but rather is only in the heart, and the passion is the torment being experienced by the person. It's not the outward excitement you are showing to others about something else.

The team-type spirit of things can be an outward sign of our true passion when it matches what is in our heart, but don't wrongly believe that if we *pretend* to be excited that it is actual true passion. This is very critical in prayer and also critical when we give thanks to the Creator who is the Most High God. If you are only acting passionate but do not actually have that passion in your heart, then your outward signs are a fraud and only serve to damage your praise or prayer giving it less value—if any value at all. When speaking to the Creator, let the passion of your heart match the team-type spirit as the words of your actual spirit flow through your lips by the whisper of your breath.

Let Your Spirit Speak

Our mouths speak a lot, but often that overrides the voice of our actual spirit. We live in a world that is in a constant state of noise coming at us from all directions all day every day, and if we don't quiet ourselves we tend to get caught up in this noise. This is why having a few moments of solitude each day is important for us. That solitude can come as we clean up alone in the bathroom as we prepare ourselves for work, it can be as we wake and all is silent in the house, or it can be at a time that we specifically take a few moments to clear our minds of the daily clutter. Find a few moments of silence for yourself each day.

Distancing ourselves from the noise of life allows us to tune in to our spirit rather than being only tuned in to the incessant noise of life. The noise of life can be anything, but think of this example: You're happy with life and all is well and then you get drawn down a path of some particular *thing* you decided you want and you become distracted and may actually add that *thing* to your prayer requests. This isn't necessarily wrong, but it is noise. Sure, we can become passionate about such *things,* but your true spirit isn't truly concerned about the car you drive or the house you have, or other such things. These things are fine, but our passions are truly connected to things of the spirit, and those things are long-term—a house is not.

Let your spirit speak when talking to God and let your true passions and true desires flow in priority to the unimportant noisy parts of life. It's when we can overcome the noise and tap into our true spirit that we can take our true passion along with some of that good noise, and then properly form it in to a proper request and "ask in My name and do not doubt." This is when our prayers make it to the Creator and are not rejected as "a stench in the nostrils" of God.

Tell the Spirit

When we have finally tapped into our own true spirit and talk to the Creator, we can then ponder our thoughts and verbalize them at normal volume or in the whisper of the spirit, but sometimes that's all we are doing.

If you want to talk to someone in your family or a friend, you typically say it directly to them in some form. This is especially true when it's something important or very dear to your heart. When it's very important to us we might even somewhat rehearse in our mind, or possibly aloud. But while our rehearsal might be helpful to us to form our thoughts clearly in our head, if we never deliver the message to them in their presence, then they will never hear our message.

Whether we are giving thanks to God for something or are asking for something from God, we must step into the presence of the Creator. I feel confident in saying that few of us realize that this is important. And even those who acknowledge the importance might not even really realize that they actually do this. For them it is more accidental or habitual than it is deliberate. When you have prayer or praise and thanks to offer to The Creator, step into the presence of God and bow your spirit before the face of God, and then state your passion. If we fail to do this it's more like when we only *practice* something important that we intend to say to a friend or family member, but then never actually deliver that message. Don't misunderstand this to mean that you shouldn't practice, because the "practice" part can be very helpful to us. In the book *Understanding Prayer* this was not referred to as "practicing", but rather it was pointed out that making things clear in our own mind *before* we pray is very important to us. So before we approach the Creator, it's good for us ourselves to have clarity of mind so that we ourselves understand what we are requesting, or for that matter what we are actually grateful for as we thank God.

What is Spirit?

What is "Spirit" anyway? Spirit is one of those things that is a concept so simple that it's difficult to describe. One of the closest analogies is air, wind, and breath which are all essentially the same thing. They're all silent, invisible, and can't be touched or held the same as when we hold an object. Sure, we can hold out our hand and in it sits air, and we can blow that air with more air from our breath and feel it in our hand, but we can't see it, yet it is still there.

Our spirit is our conscious or awareness and it will live on after our body turns to dust whether we choose to believe this or not. The essence of us is our spirit and when our breath leaves our body so does our spirit. This is the biggest reason that wind and spirit are associated—they are both there, but they cannot be seen.

When the Creator Breathed the Breath of Life into Adam, Adam's spirit came alive and his conscious began to become aware. And when Adam eventually died he took his last breath and then his Created spirit left his body. When he drew his last breath the spirit no longer was in his body, yet his spirit still exists.

Spirit is the best representation of our soul or our conscious, and God the Creator is Pure Spirit alone, which is why we often find it difficult to communicate with God. Communication issues are **our** problem, not God's problem. We are given all of the required tools to commune with the Creator, but we fail to use them properly. We have been given a body for representation, a voice for stating intention, and desire for passion. And with those gifts we can and should make requests, but we should also offer praise and thanks to God!

Chapter 6

Sticking with It

This chapter has some similarities to the *Rise Up When Times Get Tough* chapter, but "*Sticking with It*" doesn't pertain to only standing strong through tough times. Sometimes we might lose interest because something is taking too long, or we just simply lose interest. We often see this sort of thing in our children when they jump from one interest to another.

It's not necessarily a bad thing that our current point of interest jumps from one thing to another, but it can be irritating for the parents of children who do this. This lack of focus is usually done by people who have very active minds and it is our job as parents to help them better focus that energy. This is no different in our own relationship to God.

When we keep approaching God and asking for one thing this week, and then an opposing thing next month, it has to be somewhat annoying to God and can affect our own results with what we have already been given. If you actually make it into the presence of God with your requests and have those requests answered and you then change your mind, the changes in direction might render what you have already been given to be useless to you, resulting in what you had been given no longer having any value to you.

Imagine you listening to someone talking about their excitement about something, and somehow you are able to line things up for them so that they can achieve the goals and desires that they expressed at the time. Now imagine that you did a bunch of work and actually had everything in alignment and ready for them to walk into your gift, but at the last minute they decide that they have changed their mind, and what they spoke of previously is not what they want now. They completely change direction and begin to speak excitedly about something completely new and unrelated, rendering everything that you had prepared for them to now be useless to them. This would probably be very irritating to you and would likely cause you to be reluctant to prepare such a gift for them in the future.

When we jump around in our desires, we typically don't notice what we have been given regarding our previous desires, and so we never even give any thanks to God for what had been given to us regarding those previous now abandoned desires. Be aware that this occurs and has likely occurred in your own life. Make sure that the next time you enter into the presence of the Creator that you offer thanks and also probably an apology for the unused, but *answered*, prayers that you likely have not even been noticing.

Don't Give Up

It's easy to give thanks when things are going great, but not so easy when we're in the midst of tough times. We can ask in prayer for things to be rectified, but we must first make sure that *we ourselves* are not causing our own troubles. If we are doing something to bring troubles on ourself, then it is very important to examine our own life and situation. Examining our own life helps us to make some simple changes and follow basic actions that we can do on our own but that are not able to easily remedy a troubled situation. All too often, whether we cause our problems on our own, or if the world is just dealing us a hard blow, we weaken and give up. But what we need to do is to stand strong in our goals and persevere. We must examine our motives and our goals to make sure that they are always pure and will build up and create, rather than tearing down and destroying.

When we're certain that we are on the right path and we have presented our intentions to the Creator, then we must stand strong and *not* doubt. It is our doubt that causes us to waver and change direction. Our changes in direction are very irritating for people who we work with if we are giving them ever-changing instructions. Someone can waste a whole week of their life working feverishly on some whim of a superior in a company, only to have that work be made useless by a simple change in direction. This makes that week of work have little value to them and steals away the worker's contribution to the world. So their work may have been perfectly carried out, but that single small change renders it mostly worthless other than the learning experience and pay that they gained through doing the work.

Plan well first *and then* bring those plans before the Creator with true passion. The planning is like the practice spoken of in the last chapter where we must come to full realization *ourselves* before asking for assistance in our desires. When we approach God during the planning period of our desires, we should first be requesting *inspiration* and *focus* until we well understand our own end goals and have those goals fully formed in our mind so that our mental pathway is made clear. Then after we give thanks for all of that, we can ask for assistance on the more specific needs. The Creator wants us to create *good* in the world and build up, and it is those *good* requests that will be answered in their own way.

United We Stand

Christ said "Where two or three are gathered there I will be in their midst". When we work together for good, we have far greater power than when we stand alone.

If you're creating something new you might find it hard to gather *any* people who will have enough faith in your endeavors, making it difficult to gather anyone to you as a supporter when you are beginning. Interestingly enough though, once you have accomplished your goal in the successful creation of something new and great, you then will find that many will gather to you in support. This can sting a bit during the creation process, but then you get to reap your harvest as people are drawn to you and to your work. When we stand together, our strength is greatly increased. If you want to move a heavy object you might not be able to budge it on your own, but with the assistance of one other person it can be easily moved.

If you're doing something grand that few, if any, have enough faith in and you find *one* person who truly believes in your work, then give thanks to them and to God for them. People who are willing to contribute to your grand desires for your good creations in a substantive way are truly a gift and it is very important to thank God for them and for their assistance.

Nailed It!

When we reach the pinnacle of achievement and see our desires succeed it can be rewarding beyond compare. However, many of us are never able to experience that because we quit too early due to the fact that we don't want to go through all of the work or the tough times that our desires can bring during the creating process.

Too many of us tend to think that the Creator just said "let there be" and then POOF! there was a star. But the reality is that it likely took the Creator a long time to figure these things out, and it probably took a long time for the stars to be formed after things were figured out. Imagine the feeling of accomplishment when the Creator invented light–and it worked! We think the light bulb is a great invention, but imagine the invention of the actual light that a light bulb emits. If the Creator had a body like us at that time, then that body might have been jumping for joy for a long time relative to what would be in our human terms shouting "I nailed it, I nailed it!"

We get excited about the great things we invent or accomplish, but imagine the excitement of Creating the heavens and the earth. We often look to the heavens and see all of the stars but we fail to realize that those were made–and each star must be thought of as a sun much like our Sun. That's pretty grand Creating! When we do amazing things, we like to share our news with friends or even anyone who might be willing to listen to us. But the Creator could not share this joy until other beings existed. So remember, next time you get excited about your projects, know that it is truly a gift to have people with whom to share your excitement, and let us not forget that, beforehand, God made those people exist who we are now able to share our news with. We really do owe much thanks to God, and let us not forget that the Creator also wants to see our excitement! Make sure to share your excitement with God and give thanks each and every day!

Should We Cling to God?

Our foundation is important, but we have to somehow cling to that foundation. If our house is built on solid ground it is much more difficult for the rains of trouble to wash away our foundation, but if the deluge is intense enough then our foundation might stand but *we* will be washed away in the floods of trouble.

We must *attach* ourselves to that foundation, and for us humans we can do that partly through accepting Christ's nails from the Cross. When we fully accept Christ and the Cross and his Resurrection it secures our place with God provided that we live rightly, but we also need to *cling* to God to actually live rightly.

There's a lot of talk about—Salvation coming through faith—and there's truth to that, but you can believe all you want that faith will save you, yet if you keep falling short and doing cruel things you cannot expect that you will be "saved". Christ told people to "Go, and sin no more."

When we stay close to God we have a unique protection against our own foolhardy errors in that we make a whole lot less of them because we are guided by God rather than by the world.

So yes, we should cling to God with all of our might like a young child who is afraid clings to their parent because they know that parent will protect them.

Where Two or Three Are Gathered

As we gather together in our endeavors and passions, we should give thanks for those around us. Let us stand together and realize that The Christ is in our midst. This Truth cannot be denied, and when we are in Truth ourselves we then have great power to accomplish our desires. It is these times when we "ask in My name" that our pure prayers can reach the Creator "as a sweet fragrance" and be accepted.

Our true heart determines whether our praise offerings and requests are "a stench in the nostrils" or will "rise up as a sweet fragrance". Cain and Abel, the first two sons of Adam and Eve, both made offerings to God. Abel's offerings were pure and were accepted, but Cain's offerings were not pure of heart and were done more for show as a competitive offering, and so due to Cain's intent his offerings were not accepted like Able's were.

This is like when The Christ said that the poor widow woman at the temple who gave her last two bits had given more value than those who gave from their abundance but gave a lot more money than did the widow. It was the purity of humble trust that the woman had that was so valued by God, rather than the pomp of arrogance offered by some others.

When we give thanks to God it should be done in a manner of humility. Not meaning that you must feel lowly, but let's take note of exactly Who we are talking to here. Reverence and pure passion of spirit with true sincerity are what the Creator wants from us most of all, and then for us to take that and ask for good things with it, and then *do* good things with it.

When we get this right and we are gathered in "my name", then we humans have an enormous ability to positively affect our own life and the lives of those around us. This allows us to make a positive contribution to the entire world, even if that contribution is only local to us.

Chapter 7

Prayer and Praise Are Different

When addressing God, realize in your own heart that *praise* and *prayer* are two entirely different points. *Praise* is to give Glory to God, where *prayer* is more connected to requesting something *from* the Creator. If you're already doing both then it's not as critical that you realize that there's a difference between the two words, but it is still personally important to us that we all understand the difference between the two concepts of *praising* versus *praying*.

When we don't distinguish between these two concepts then we do a whole lot more asking and very little thanking and Glorifying of God. But when we understand that there is a difference between *prayer* and *praise* then we are more aware and are more likely to give Glory to God who, as the Creator of all things, certainly deserves praise and Glory from us for nothing more than Creation itself. And then add to that, the fact that we also have many of our prayers answered for which we owe a deep debt of gratitude. But let us not forget that while we might not notice it, we are also being protected from much darkness and toil even in our sometimes-troubled lives. You need not look far to see people who are worse off than are you—and as is often said, "But for the Grace of God there go I."

Divided We Fall

In the last chapter, the importance of standing united and "sticking with it" were discussed. For the most part, we humans do stand together, and when we do, we have great strength. We see this on full display in our political world, where the darker factions of politics have an ability to stand together no matter how wrong they are, and through their unity they are able to accomplish much of the destruction they so desperately seek to invoke upon the rest of us. These darker factions have mastered the art of division of their opponents while drawing to themselves many of their opponents that they previously divided and were made to believe that they were misfits.

The good people of this world are not loud-mouthed people. We all just shut up and do our work while not wanting to infringe upon the rights of others. But the darker factions of politics understand that if they attack us individually, or attack our small groups, they will potentially succeed in dividing us. They are like wild beasts on the hunt who divide their prey so that they can conquer and kill that prey one at a time. They themselves feel that they have no real value, so the only thing they can do is to attempt to bring others lower than they feel that they themselves are by forcing us to succumb to their evil demands.

But what we don't see is that if we cling to God and stand together in the large group that we actually are, then they will be trampled underfoot by our resolve. Those of us who believe in God understand that if we cling to the Creator who Created all things we would rarely or never be able to be overcome by evil and darkness if good people would simply stick together. Evil will always attempt to destroy and defame innocent and good people in effort to separate them into ever smaller groups in attempt to "Go in for the kill."

Do not lose faith when evil rears its ugly head. Stand strong on your foundation and do not allow yourself to be divided from the Creator or from your good fellow man who also clings to God.

Separation Can Be Good

When we're internally divided we can be more readily defeated, which is a matter of the division of heart and spirit. Finding time to step away from others periodically to get alone-time to clear your mind is important to you personally. Brief solitude can be good in cases of internal division to just relax and hear the voice of God.

We also have the separation of *issues* to consider, like realizing that *prayer* and *praise* are two completely different concepts. Our minds are a wonderful gift from the Creator and we need to exercise them with understanding. If we are unable to separate out two simple concepts like *prayer* and *praise*, then similar confusion is most certainly occurring in many other areas of our lives causing us untold grief, and we won't even realize it.

For instance, our understanding of the Bible's Creation account in Genesis chapter one is full of separation issues that we miss, and therefore we **mis**interpret the Creation account in many ways as is detailed in the *The Science of God Volumes*. When we miss these critical points of separation it allows us to believe outright lies and be deceived. We must understand *separation*, and then keep together that which is good, and separate that which is bad. Our ability to *separate* is of immense value to us, and it enters every part of our lives with no part untouched by the concept of *separation*. We have separation of ideas which allows us to see more clearly, but we also have separation of people and values which can be good or bad depending upon who you're separating from and what it is that they believe.

Let not yourself be separated from God, because that is the one separation that is sure to bring your imminent destruction. Give thanks, praise, honor, and Glory to God at all times.

Making More with Less

If you're suffering because the world seems to be dealing you an unfair hand in life, then realize that another person in your situation could come out of that same situation more quickly because they know exactly what to do to remedy the problems at hand. It is their *understanding* that allows them to progress. Getting this notion firmly in your mind can be of great service to you, because then *you* understand that there is a way for you to pass through the river of troubles that is trying to sweep you away.

It would be easy for a rich man to overcome the same problems that a poor man has, because money can typically buy the needed items or pay the fees to solve many problems. Yet, even if you took all of the money from that rich man, if he is one who created his riches on his own rather than having inherited it, he could likely easily solve the problems due to his past experiences and quickly regain much wealth if he lost the original wealth.

There are ways to do things when you have very little to work with. Take the example given in the Bible where Christ tells the parable of the three men whose master left them to tend to some of his wealth. When the rich master left, each of three men were given an amount of money to care for. Two of the servants made the money work for the master and had more when he returned, but the other servant buried the money because he did not want to risk losing it because he was afraid of what might happen if he lost it. When the master returned, he referred to the man who buried the money as a "wicked and lazy servant". The master then gave that servant's money to one of the other servants to care for because they would at the very least get some interest from that money for the master.

We have what we have, including our gifts and good desires. Will we bury those like the "wicked and lazy servant" that Christ told the story about? Or will we make what little we have grow and flourish? God wants us to succeed and is joyful regarding our individual situation only when we take our good talents and make them grow and prosper. Make the most you can of what little you have, especially during the hard times when life really stings. Our value to the Creator is greatly increased when we do so, just like the woman that gave her last two bits.

Multiplying Your Praise

As you find your true good passions and begin to use them, then inspiration will abound in your heart, mind, and in your desires. But when we have given ourselves over to the world, then our true passions and desires often conflict with our worldview. This causes us to have to make some hard changes so that we are no longer burying our talents in the ground like the wicked and lazy servant.

When you release your true and good passions and desires then your ability to offer praise and thanksgiving to the Creator becomes more joyous and more abundant. It is easier to give thanks when things are going good. But when those tough times come it is also very important to glorify God. This is because praising God tends to gain momentum in our lives and in our hearts, and then life tends to get easier for us. And the easier it gets then the easier it is to remember to praise God. When God is our primary focus, then the better things get for us the more joy we feel, making it ever easier to offer authentic and true glory and praise and thanks to God.

Just as the two servants increased their master's money, so too is our praise multiplied when we use it rather than burying it.

Our Separation of Good and Evil

In our youth we might have heard the Garden of Eden story and thought that Adam and Eve were given knowledge in the Garden when they ate from the tree. In fact there are many of us adults who assume that this is what happened. The Serpent tempted Eve, and then Eve ate of the fruit of the Tree of Knowledge, but there's a little more to the story than that. Adam and Eve did not eat from the Tree of Knowledge of *everything*— they ate of the Tree of Knowledge of *Good* and *Evil*. It was at that point in time that Adam and Eve were able to tell the difference between *good* and *evil*. Before that point they could have done pretty much anything and would not have been found guilty because of their innocence in not understanding that there is a difference between *good* and *evil*. But when they chose to follow the wrong master they then made themselves subordinate to that master, and their new-found ability to differentiate good and evil was passed down to all of us—*we* are their descendants. In doing so they made themselves subordinate to the evil one, thus causing death to come to themselves and all of us—their grandchildren.

Our human ability to determine *good* and *evil* can be seen in very young children when they see something evil that us foolish adults make that is graphically grotesque. Even an innocent child of only several months old can detect intended evil in most such cases. This ability to tell between good and evil is also very apparent with toddlers when they color on the walls and partake in other such two-year-old antics. All we need to do is ask, "who colored on the wall?" and they will typically go straight into denial or finger pointing to the actual instigator or the accomplices, much as Adam and Eve did in the Garden when God did nothing more than ask the simple question of them—"Where art thou?"

Our ability to *separate* allows us to discern between good and evil, and through that discernment we can choose our own path. We have truly achieved free-will, even unto our own destruction if we so choose. But we also can choose to commune with God and offer our praises and thanks-giving to the Most High God.

Chapter 8

In My House

Ever since the time of Creation, mankind has been able to live in a house of God, that is to say the Earth. Not that God lives on the Earth like we do, but the Earth is the property of the Creator and we were put on Earth to care for it.

The Earth is Our Vessel

Just as your house is likely a point of pride and a place of safety for you and your family, so too is the Earth to God and a place of safety for us. Imagine a friend or neighbor coming into your home and destroying parts of it or thinking that *they* best know how much light you need in your home, so they cover your windows with boards, all without your permission.

For most of us, we would promptly ask them to leave and we would show them to the door. *We* are responsible for our homes, both the wood-and-nails boxes we live in and the vessel we call "Earth" as well as our bodies.

We must all care for our own part of Earth that we are charged with while we are alive. We should plant it and make it beautiful by giving more to it than we take from it. We think of ourselves as living on the Earth but we actually live inside of the Earth because our atmosphere is as much a part of our planet as is the dirt under our feet is. If we attempted to live outside of our atmosphere we would need special equipment to breathe or we would promptly meet our end.

Earth is a vessel that we in our human understanding can think of as a protective spaceship that reliably carries us around the Sun without fail at tens of thousands of miles per hour every minute of every day of every year. It's really quite amazing, but we're so accustomed to it that we rarely take the time to consider any of this.

If any one of us was suddenly cast into space just above our atmosphere, without any special breathing equipment or a space suit then we would quickly realize just how wonderful our environment is, and how special this spaceship we call Earth is. Just as a ship sailing the oceans is a vessel, so too is our Earth that protects us and carries us as it circles our Sun. Let us all acknowledge the magnificence of this and express that acknowledgment with passion of true spirit to the Creator, The Most High God.

The Vessels We Are

When we're born, we are born in the vessel of our human mother. And her womb is the space in which we are created by her according to the instruction given by the Creator. As we grow, we all become vessels ourselves, and our body-vessels will be filled with our spirit and all that we learn.

As parents, we must take great care in what we allow to flow into the vessels of our children. Will we allow their spirit to be contaminated with darkness and evil, or will we fill them with the Light of Truth? You can be certain that they will be filled with something, but as a parent of young children **you** get to decide what you are going to allow to flow into them. The same is true for ourselves: Will we allow evil into our spirit, our will we keep our spirit lighted with the purity of Truth?

Our Purpose is to Be Filled

Our bodies are not some random act of evolution. Our bodies are very specifically designed with the purpose of being filled with our spirit, and that spirit is made aware through the interface of our body.

So as we fill our spirit, we must realize that even if we don't want to fill ourselves with anything, the body *will* be filled with something regardless. But *we* have the gift of being able to *choose* what specifically we will allow into these body vessels. If we are not aware of the void within ourself where Truth is meant to reside, then we are also not aware that we are likely being filled with evil.

Will we allow ourselves to be complacent, and through that allow evil into our spirit, contaminating our spirit to a point of no return? The time is now to fill ourselves with Truth before it's too late. There's a point that redemption is no longer available to us, and if we cross that bridge we will feel the murky flames in the end.

Your purpose is to be filled. You are a vessel made of clay and you are supposed be filled with the Light of Truth. When we allow God's Holy Spirit to live in us, we have accomplished the greatest tribute to God that we possibly can. But if we deny this Truth, then ours is a bitter end that will last very long.

Let us all be grateful that we each can choose to fill ourselves with goodness and Truth and that we can become the light to guide others to that same Truth so that they too may become filled with the Spirit of Light. We will be filled no matter what, but what will we allow ourselves to be filled with? Will we contaminate our spirit and have Truth flee far from us? Or will we embrace Truth and let it overflow in us and spill out for others to see?

Under My Roof and Within My Walls

It's a bit ironic how we'll protect our house with violence if need be to try to keep bad things away from our home. But when it comes to our body, we do things like permanently painting them with graffiti and punching holes all over them, and worse, we allow evil into us by the entertainment and sometimes by the friends we choose. Always keep in mind that we must live with our choices the remainder of our lives.

Your body is yours to do with what you choose, but never forget that those choices all have consequences for both the good things we do to ourselves *and* for the bad things we do to ourselves. And we will pay a price for the negative influence we have on others. What you keep in your mind can either be like a garden of joy that flourishes, or it can be a thicket of briars, thorns, and weeds causing punctures, blisters, and pain.

Protect your vessel and only allow good within you and only partake in things that are good for you. Do not invite evil and destruction in—keep those far from you. Allow Truth in you and let it fill you completely. Understand Truth and know it well. It is the foundation of all things, and with it you can achieve great things. Anyone who has truly achieved this state of being will understand this and they understand the power that it gives them to succeed in the endeavors connected to the good desires of their heart. Let your body-vessel be your personal protector by choosing well with proper discernment as you utilize the Truth that you were originally born with. The Bible has been telling us for thousands of years to realize that **we** get to make choices about allowing Truth within us, but too few of us have ever read the Bible cover-to-cover in effort to find these things out, thus most of us do not know this.

Let your spirit control your body and all actions that your body takes so that it may be your protector along with the Spirit of the Creator. With good choices you can make your body walk away from evil and darkness and then walk only towards the Glory of God.

Thanks from Within

Earlier we discussed letting the whisper of our breath speak to God in praise and thanksgiving while quietly but audibly speaking to God with the understanding that this is more *for us to hear ourselves* than it is for God to hear us. Not only should we verbalize our prayers and praises to the Creator, but we must also offer thanks from within.

We can praise the Creator at any point in time with our soul in the privacy of our own body. When we face times of trouble and get caught up in unwanted confusion with other people, we still have the ability to praise the Most High God as we endure the pain of the situation. This does not mean that we must say "thank you for this trouble", but rather we can thank God and offer praise that we know we will be guided out of the situation when we adhere to Truth. We can also thank God for what we learn during our troubled times.

Our internal praise, if it is honest and true, has a tendency to show in our disposition, demeanor, on our face, and in our body language. If we're more relaxed, other people are generally more accommodating to us than if we have the inconfidence of doubt and fear on our faces or in our actions.

One of the big secrets of success that is often fraudulently duplicated is *confidence*. But if you do not have Truth within you then your "confidence" is more along the lines of *arrogance*. When we fall for someone's arrogance and accept it as if it is true confidence, then we typically get wholly or partially drawn into their lies and contaminate our own body vessel and spirit.

Near constant praise to God from within is very good for our health and for our lives. It increases the good chemistry within the body and gives us a better appearance to others. We often run around with a look of worry or concern on our faces as we hurry and scurry about to our next daily task, causing us to come across as cranky or unfriendly. But when we learn to praise from within, we can learn to praise in a near constant state even as we do other things without it causing us any distraction. It becomes as if it is breathing where it just happens without us having to think about it. Work to offer thanks from within whenever you are reminded to think about it, and eventually it becomes a habit that can change your appearance to an appearance of joy. Doing so will change your life!

Chapter 9

Embrace Thy Self

Second to the Creator, *you* are important to *you*. Obviously the Creator is more important to you than you yourself are because without the Creator nothing would **be**–including you. But *you* are very important to *you* above all else. If you had never been born then you would not *be* and so you wouldn't matter. But you are here and you're reading this, making it evident that you are a spirit *being* in the body-vessel that belongs to you.

Accept yourself as a unique individual and embrace yourself for what you are. You were Created with *purpose* and for *good* to dwell with God's Great Spirit as a companion to explore and see and share in all of Creation.

Too many of us claim that we dislike ourselves and we go out of our way to prove it. We also pretend that we're someone else by copying their foolish actions or behavior, thus following them down their path to destruction, and in doing so we're nothing but cheap and poor imitations of fools.

We have been Created in perfect Light and that Light is for all of mankind, and it's not just for some of us—it's for all of us. We must choose the light deliberately, but we cannot choose that light when we have chosen to hate ourselves.

We are worthy and have great value to the Creator when we accept the Light of Truth. But if we have chosen the path of self-hatred then the further down that path we go, the more difficult it is for us to come back. This compounds itself as we travel on either path. The more we draw near to the Light then the more power we have to overcome the darkness. Conversely, the more we draw to the darkness, then the less power we have to escape the grasp of darkness.

When we understand our own true place and true value we are then embracing ourselves, and then the Light of Truth will dwell within us, thus increasing our value to the Creator and to the World. Every one of us has this gift within our grasp and all we need to do is to grab hold of the Light and never let it go.

Protect Thy Self

You are important to yourself and it's your job as an adult to protect yourself and not allow evil into you. When we read or watch things that are not of God, we then compromise ourselves and will eventually pay a price for this to some extent because we are all affected by that which we see and hear and experience. When we choose to indulge ourselves with things of darkness we are inviting more darkness into our lives. It seems like it would be easy to avoid such darkness and evil, but darkness comes into our lives disguised as desirous and as goodness, and when it can, it attempts to present itself as light.

When stories and movies are written and invented that portray evil and darkness as good, and we indulge ourselves in such hidden-evil-stories, then those written ideas will slowly weaken our spirit making it more difficult to see darkness the next time we encounter it. This is especially dangerous to our children when we allow them to indulge in such evil-disguised-as-good entertainment. As we slowly become desensitized to darkness we lose sight of the Light of Truth, and in doing so we give the darkness all power over us. Once we reach this point it becomes very difficult for us to escape the grasp of darkness. Our only way out is to reject darkness and embrace the Light of Truth.

We are protected by the Light of Truth and we owe God a great deal of thanks for that protection. Draw near to the Light of Truth and never let go. Remove the darkness from your own life so that you may be a beacon of hope to those who are trapped in the pull of darkness. It is the joy and hope that the Light of Truth brings us that allows those who have succumbed to darkness to see the Light that shines from within us. This helps us to find our way out of the darkness in which we have trapped ourselves.

Into Thy Bosom

When a child is afraid of the dark or has been hurt, the most comforting thing for them is when they are being held close and firm by their mother. The father is of great comfort as well, but there is something very special about very young children being held in the bosom of their mother. There is great value and great meaning in this embrace and we can learn a lot from it. The relationship between parent and child is an analogy of the relationship between God and us. The sooner we see this then the more we can learn from it as we live our lives.

The protection by our parents and the protection of our selves gives us a clue as to how we are protected by God when we embrace the Light of Truth.

Dear Lord Hold Me

When we're weary from our struggles, we need to reach up to God and ask the Creator to hold us firmly. Let your fears rest in the arms of God and let God wipe away your tears. There's great comfort in handing over our worries to God and asking for protection. We sometimes misunderstand this as an attitude of— *we don't need to deal with our own problems*—but that's not at all what this means.

When we hand our troubles over to God, it is a sign of trust that things will work out and that we have no need to panic about our troubles. When we follow the Light of Truth then all things will be taken care of in their own time and clear paths will be revealed to us. It is *our* choice to choose those right paths

God typically doesn't do our work for us, but our inspiration does come from God's Light of Truth. And it is that inspiration that guides us out of trouble. Often the right people or opportunities are presented to us at the hand of God, but when we are not protected by God we are typically blind to those opportunities, and thus, we miss them entirely.

Give a Great Big Hug of Thanks

Anyone who has children has probably experienced the joy of getting a *spontaneous* great big hug from their child. Even when the hug is due to something we might have given to or done for them it's still a pretty rewarding sign of love and affection!

If we connect the *things* we get or the things we have with our willingness to offer love to others, then we become focused on material goods and status and then eventually love slips away from us. True love cannot be bought; it is a gift of the spirit and heart that we freely give to others.

When we offer our gift of love to others there are some who will reject our gift and not allow us to love them. We can still try, but love is really a two-way transaction. Most of us have experienced rejection of the love that we have offered someone. Probably the most familiar is during the dating years of life when you find a person who you really like and it builds into love, but the other person did have the same strong feelings towards you. This sort of rejection is very painful for us. But with God we will never be rejected when we seek the Light of God's love.

Seek the Spirit of Truth and when you find it, hold on tightly and do not let go! Give God a great big hug of thanks and praise for all that you have. Even in hard times when our health falters or when money is tight or when we're just feeling down we must reach out to God and give God a great big hug by embracing the Light of Truth.

Kindness **To** and Love **Of** Ourself

For most people it's easy to offer kindness to *others* because that's a very important part of our God-like design and purpose, but we often struggle when being kind to *ourselves*. We tend to either feel guilty for doing good for ourselves, or we go too far down the path and we *only* think of ourselves, and then we forget those around us who may have a real need for kindness and love from us.

We are clearly promised in the Bible that when we give to God that "...it shall be given to you: good measure and pressed down and shaken together and running over shall they give into your bosom. For with the same measure that you shall measure all, it shall be measured to you again...". But due to many preachers asking for money while using this Bible quote, we tend to only see this as pertaining to money. It is true with our money, but most everything in the Bible has little to do with money and is much more focused on the Love and Truth that we should have and exhibit towards others. Money is used only as an illustrative analogy by Jesus because it's a concept that we are all familiar with and can understand.

When we love ourselves then we value ourselves and we have no need to compete with our fellow man. But if we have no true love of ourself, then self-hatred fills our spirit and we become unkind to ourself and to others while we try to fill that void with money, status, or things as we compete for a top spot with our fellow man.

If we hate ourself, then we will feel that we have no value, and the reason that some of us hate ourself is because the Light of Truth of which we have been speaking has been hidden from us or we are blind to it. When we feel lowly about ourselves we have little other choice but to withdraw into our own darkness or to try to defeat or harm others who we see as greater than us.

It is Created within us to want to be on high serving God and communing with God, but when we feel low our natural inclination is to want to try to appear higher. However, when darkness is our guide we are then incapable of reaching upward and so we unjustly attempt to bring others down instead.

This is exactly what occurred in the Garden of Eden when the Serpent tempted Eve. It was the Serpent's intent to bring Adam and Eve low because the Serpent was jealous of the position God had Created Adam and Eve in. This position caused the Serpent to see Adam and Eve as rivals to itself, and because the Serpent already had an ability to discern between good and evil it mistook Adam and Eve's position as being greater than the Serpent's. This caused the Serpent to feel lower than the Serpent had previously felt in relation to God. The only thing the Serpent could then see clearly to do was to try to cause Adam and Eve to be brought low in the eyes of God.

The Serpent wrongly compared itself to Adam and Eve rather than simply loving itself and being kind to itself in that love. We always think of the Serpent as evil and indeed the Serpent did do evil. However, that was not always the case. The serpent was once the bearer of Light, yet it forfeited that light when it tried to challenge God and bring itself equal to God.

The Creator is pure Spirit—the first and the last. Anything built on the system of Creation that the Creator made will ultimately cease without the Creator. As long as we love ourself just as we were Created, we will have kindness in our heart and love in our spirit and we will be able to share that with our fellow man.

But when we choose the path of self-hatred, our darkness hides the light from our plain view and we become arrogant and are indirectly mean to others, and sometimes directly mean to others all in effort to *appear as if* we have *risen up* to a higher level than we were Created as. Darkness offers only a false sense of worthlessness, but we all truly can defeat the darkness with a single decision in a moment of time.

When we dwell in darkness we are incapable of loving ourself and others, causing us to react in a way that is destructive to all. But when we make the decision to embrace the Light of Truth then kindness and love of one's self become natural along with kindness and love of others. This tends to make us feel more grateful for all that we have. We must remember to offer thanks to God for this and for the Light of Truth with which we all can, and all should, fill ourselves.

Chapter 10

Dedication to the End

How many times have we made some promise to God where—if only this would happen or if that would happen—but then when it happens, we somehow forget our promise or we claim that since we did it on our own we're not responsible for the promises we made?

Our dedication to our commitments is lacking in every imaginable way. We see things *our* way, do things *our* way, and want things *our* way, but we fail to see things **God's** way. We're typically more dedicated to our own folly than we are to the good that the Creator is attempting to bestow upon us.

We all really need to refocus our dedication to the commitments that we made to the Creator over the years. Re-examine your commitments and discuss them with God, making sure to do more than just *hear* God's whisper, because you also need to *listen* to that whisper.

Our Commitment

Our commitments are the things that we promise to do. But it is our dedication to those commitments that determines whether or not those commitments will ever be fulfilled by us.

Commitments are very important to us, and we tend to get very offended when other people don't meet their commitments to us. This is true in business commitments, but it is really critical in our personal commitments as well. When we have someone who we think of as "close to us" and that person breaks a commitment to us, it tends to sting quite a bit. And when it's a situation regarding commitment of love, like in family, the pain gets even greater. Now add to that the love-commitment between a man and a woman, where when that commitment is broken the pain felt is over-the-top painful.

It's important to keep our commitments, and even more important the closer those commitments are to love, with romantic love being the most sensitive. Violation of our commitments of love brings out the worst in us and in those whom we have violated our commitment to. With marriage commitment we tend to think of this breach of commitment in terms of infidelity, but infidelity can be more than just physical. Infidelity includes the breaking of *any* of the promises of marriage and intimacy. While the intimacy between man and woman is of both of a carnal nature and of a spiritual nature, the breach in either causes great pain for the offended spouse. In understanding this level of commitment, we must realize that the relationship between husband and wife is a model of the actual relationship between The Creator and us.

We might make promises to the Creator that we don't intend to keep or possibly are not capable of keeping, sort of like when the kids promise that they'll take care of the dog when we buy them a puppy. But the real commitment between us and God is our desire for Light that many of us fail to keep.

Just as a parent wants all of their children to succeed in all good things that they do, so too God wants us to succeed in obtaining the ultimate existence—which is to be filled with the Light of Truth, and then all good things will come out of that.

True Believing

The Light that guides our way allows us to achieve a different level of belief. We all believe things, but not so much that we would gamble on our belief, so really we only **kind of believe** things. Christ said "if you believe in your heart and do not doubt" then amazing things could happen. He also said that if we "had faith as small as a mustard seed", thus indicating that it doesn't take loads of faith but rather only *certain* faith.

It is not the *level* of faith, but rather it is the **quality** of faith and belief that matters. Though we believe, we are not really true believers, because if we were, then we all would be healing the sick and infirm and would be doing God's good work at all times. But instead *we kind of believe* because we have little room for Truth in us. It is when we have fully embraced Truth that we begin to understand the full purpose and value of offering our gratitude to the Creator.

If you truly believe, then you are likely going to be able to rationally explain your faith without falling back on the same old lies and inaccuracies. That is to say, the lies and inaccuracies that so many of us have believed over the years, only to have what little faith we have in us crushed by darkness.

True believing is accomplished by true commitment to the Light of Truth, and when we seek that Light and find it then it luminates our way to true believing. If we do not truly believe in the Creator who we refer to as "God", then we are being somewhat fraudulent when we pray to that God. Imagine a child asking for some small thing from a parent and then immediately after asking of the parent, the child begins doubting that the parent has the ability to fulfill the child's request. If what the child requested was actually a reasonable request, then the parent would very likely be hurt and insulted and possibly angry that the child would see the parent as lowly or incompetent as being incapable of meeting the child's simple and reasonable requests. This is exactly what we do to God in our doubt. We insult the Creator of all things seen and invisible. Our lack of faith in the Creator is hurtful, insulting, and frustrating to the Creator.

There is Work to Be Done

Our commitments require work on our part and we must work more diligently to fulfill our commitments. If a builder commits to build you a home and you're paying for it, then that builder has a great deal of work to do in order to fulfill his part of the commitment, while all you have to do is to write out a check for the work being done.

In our relationship to God we are the ones who owe for the work that the Creator *has already done* and we repay the Creator by using our true gifts and talents. So not only do we get the benefits of Creation, but we also get to pay the Creator back by using the gifts we have been given. This is a very good deal for us when we actually utilize our talents rather than burying them like the wicked and lazy servant Christ spoke of that was mentioned in a previous chapter.

Of course, life with its unfair kicks tries to stop us from using those talents, and so we end up contributing to our fellow man while struggling to do things that are not of our own gifted talents. Some parts of life are mere stepping stones to get us to where we ought to be, but we often become complacent and fail to ever move on, only to endure a lackluster life, never moving beyond that first or second stepping stone.

When we begin to experience joy in life we can know that we're getting close to our best paths, but let us not confuse joy with happiness. Joy is typically a deliberate result of doing the right things, where happiness is not always repeatable and typically occurs due to chance.

As we offer thanks and praise to God, we must all realize that not only do we all have to work on ourselves to improve ourselves and our understanding of what is true, but we also must contribute to our communities through our work. This is not referring to charity, rather it is about you using your gifts to support yourself and increase the world *at the same time*. These efforts and outward actions become examples of the way to live for our children and for those around us. Let us all make sure that the examples we set are good ones.

We Shall Prevail

Our commitments, and our dedication to those commitments, are what allow us to accomplish our goals. We certainly have commitments to our fellow man and to God, but we also have commitments to ourselves. We have desires and we make plans to fulfill those desires, but too often we shoot for the stars and then feel like we have failed because we didn't meet our desired level of our end goal, thus causing us to give up completely. Sometimes when we set our sights very high in this way, or even too high, we might fall short of those specific goals, but we still actually achieve a great deal more than most people do.

We will prevail when we stick with it and continue on even though we might not completely reach our full desired end goal. What we have accomplished, we have accomplished, and no one can strip us of the fact that we accomplished a great deal even though it is not the pinnacle of what we might have been trying to achieve.

Let us never allow fools to devalue any contributions that we did make. And let us give thanks that we were able to contribute to the world as we have been able.

We Can Add to It

As we feel the disappointment of not having reached our goals we must always realize that life is not over as long as we still have the breath of life within us.

Our lives are not something that is dependent on some specified goal that we feel we must meet by a certain date. It is certainly good to set such time goals for ourselves, but not so that we must commiserate and get depressed if we miss those goals. Life is robust and will live on no matter what we personally accomplish, so if we choose to quit then we have made our choice to bury our talents and be a "wicked and lazy servant". As long as we continue to contribute and increase society in some large or small way, we are doing our job. If we happen to meet our intended goals, then that's great. Our goals do change, so it's very important to understand that you **are** allowed to modify or change your goals. If we have a personal goal and miss the target deadline that we committed to, then we have to realize that we can always add to our work time-goal and extend our personal deadline.

We humans tend to try to package everything into our own little mental compartments, and so, we become inflexible to a point where we are not able to see that there are other options. Most things do not fit into the pretty little packages that we try to mentally force them into.

We can always add to our goals and desires, and we can *always* modify them when needed. With each step in our path towards those good end-goals we have made the world just a little bit better. We can also add to the praise we offer to God with each step we take.

Chapter 11

Be Ready to Receive It

Many of us are guilty of rejecting *good* gifts from God. When stating that we are "guilty" of this, it is not intended to mean that it's wrong for us to decline a gift, but rather that is it foolish to decline a gift *from God*.

We often get caught off-guard when good things come to us because we're accustomed to having to work very hard for what we get. Often, good things do come to us and we fail to accept and embrace them, but when something bad comes to us we quickly accept it as a "normal" or as an acceptable part of life. What we need to do is to reject bad things and be ready to accept good things in our hearts. When bad comes to us we have this, "*oh, that's just the way life is*" attitude, and it is true that life is often unfair, but we need to reject any unfairness and *overcome it*, rather than just accepting the barrage of unfairness that often comes our way. Overcoming unfairness is how successful people actually succeed.

Our ability to receive *good* is our best defense against the unfair aspects of life that come at us. When we ready ourselves to receive *good* then it can come to us. Open your heart to receive *good* from God and give thanks for that ability.

We Need to Listen

Listening is a skill that most of us lack. We all have lots to say, but we usually fail to listen properly. Listening is a valuable skill that we all need to master. Most troubles in the world come from our *not* listening. We often say to someone "Yes, I heard you", but *hearing* is different than *listening*. When we hear someone it's a mechanical function of the body where the sound vibration in the air travels into our ear causing our eardrum to vibrate thus sending signals to our brain where that sound is being received so that we can interpret it–But that is *not* "listening".

"Listening" includes the mechanical aspects of hearing *and* the *processing* of the information *without disregarding it*. If we don't mentally process the information that we heard, then we are not listening. It is our *full consideration* that is inherent in the *listening process* that gives us an ability to make wise choices.

It's pretty obvious in our design that we are made to *receive*. Our eyes take in visual stimuli, our ears hear, our nose can sense fragrance, our skin can feel touch, and our mouths can taste and eat. But our outward communication is mostly limited to our movements and voice.

Our design speaks to the importance for us to *listen more* than we speak or act in response to what we hear. It seems a pretty safe assumption that if we were supposed to send out more than we receive, that we would be able to send physical communication beyond movement and voice. But since our inputs outweigh our outputs, it is a clear sign of the importance of our need to listen carefully and then *properly process the input*.

We generally only associate listening with voice and the hearing of that voice, but listening is really more than just hearing. When someone is trying to get us to understand something that we are just not getting the point of, then a great deal of their expression comes in their body movements which is sensed by us through our vision. Or when a parent spanks a child for doing wrong, that action is felt by the child via the child's rear-end. The parent is trying to get a message through to the child when they *properly moderately* spank their child. When we fail to listen, it frustrates those who are trying to get the point across to us.

Listening is very important and most of us are very bad at it—this is especially true when it comes to listening to God. When in prayer and praise we are generally yapping, telling God all of the good things we want in our lives, or more often, which problems we want fixed or to be made better. But how often do we quiet our minds *and just listen* for that calm quiet whisper from God?

Are We Open?

Because we have not learned the skill of *listening*, we have closed ourselves off from the Light of Truth, and it is this Light that is the key to our joy. Few of us are *truly open* to those around us or to the Creator of the Universe.

Our closed-minded attitudes have gotten so terrible that many of us will only believe what we choose to believe rather than the truth about any topic at hand. The dichotomy of things like trying to make it a felony to be cruel to an animal which could allow varying interpretations of "cruelty", versus the encouragement of the legalization of abortion, or more frankly put—the murder of human babies—is a real problem with our minds. Are we really "open" when we want to make it a felony to be cruel to an animal, but the murder of an innocent baby still in the womb is thought to be an acceptable sick sort of virtue?

We humans will suffer a great deal so long as we remain in our closed-minded attitudes. This foolish nature has occurred through our acceptance of darkness that began in the Garden of

Eden. It is only the Light of Truth that makes us able to escape this path of darkness.

Most of us have been the subject of or have witnessed when someone won't listen to sound reasoning, and that is where we also have problems. If we rationalize something without the Light of Truth being present, then our rationalizing is sure to be faulty. But when our rationalization is based solely on the process of Truth, then the rationale will make sense to everyone who has *not* abandoned Truth.

Our first task is to realize that we are not open even though we were Created to be open and receive. We must actually listen and process what we receive through the filter of Truth in order to achieve any real openness.

Accepting the Facts

When we use the filter of Truth it is much easier to separate the true facts from the things we or someone else *wants* to be facts. This is where most of us really get off track and cause ourselves tremendous trouble.

What we *want* to be "fact" often does not match the actual facts, and nowhere is this more true than with our current points of interest. It's natural for us to have desires. In fact, desire is one of our strongest points and is where our passions are initially derived from. This is all good and is as it should be, but too often our desires and passion lack the wisdom that should *always* accompany them.

When we are desirous of something, then that which we are desirous of might not be good for us or anyone else because it could cause our own or other people's destruction. When we're overcome by our passion and have excessive passion for our desire, then that desire had better be of a good nature or we are sure to destroy ourselves with it. When we catch ourselves up in such destructive burning desires we are strongly inclined to ignore all reason and we then proceed to fulfill those passionate desires. Such burning desires could be for money, or things, or unrighteous carnal activity, or any other thing that can bring destruction to us.

Always do your best to listen to what others say. This does not mean that you *hear* and *obey*, but rather that you *process* and *consider* their comments to see if those comments meet with Truth. Be open to hearing other points of opinion, especially when they do not agree with your own. It is when others challenge our own ideas that we can have better clarity. We might find that we were altogether wrong, but we can also see the truths in our own thoughts more clearly when our own thoughts are challenged by the erred thoughts of others.

When we're forced through the processes of the *consideration* of other people's thoughts, it causes us to have to double-check our own thoughts to see if we can prove their contrary thoughts wrong. If we cannot prove contrary thoughts wrong then we truly need to reexamine our own thoughts because we may have to accept the fact that our "facts" are potentially *not* actually **facts,** but rather are our desires that have overridden our good judgement. Discern Truth and make good judgement always.

Prepare to Receive

We can be ready to receive in our mind and we can listen and be open and accept all true fact and still not be prepared to receive it. I suppose that "being *ready* to receive" could be thought of as being *prepared* to receive, but it's different in the point being made here. With being *ready* to receive it's more of a disposition of being *willing* to receive, which many of us think we are, but we actually are not. However, once we realize this and conquer it so that we *are* ready to receive, we still need to *prepare to receive*.

You will find that preparation is always a big deal in the Bible if you read the entire book. And even though some of us have read the Bible in its entirety, we can still easily miss these simple points. Preparation and planning go hand in hand, but planning is somewhat different. You can *plan* a party but to prepare for it you have to take certain actions and actually do something.

When you *prepare* to receive you will take the needed actions to receive before the receipt of that which you are waiting to receive. For instance, if you were going to get a new comfortable bed you will likely prepare first and remove the old one before the new one arrives so that you have room for it. This is true for our body-vessel as well. If we fail to make room specifically for good things to enter into us, then some of what is in us will spill out when we allow other bad things into us, thus leaving us with less good each time we take in bad things. We must make room to receive while also filtering what we are willing to receive. In making room, our goal is to deliberately remove the bad things and then only allow good things into us.

Thy Cup Runneth Over

We were meant to be filled and we will overflow as water is being poured into us. But the question is, what will we overflow with? Will it be filthy contaminated water that inhibits and poisons us, or will it be the water of the pureness of Truth?

If we are indulging in things of darkness then the body, heart, and sprit eventually become filled with that darkness and evil, causing an overflow out of us of negativity, violence, destruction, and cruelty.

However, when we choose the Light of Truth then it is Light that will overflow from us in our attitude, words, and actions towards our fellow man, thus allowing them to witness our joy. When people see the Light of Truth flowing from you, they will be attracted to that Truth if they have not gone too far down the path of darkness. And even when they have gone too far down that dark path they will still be envious of your Light, but they will usually respond with malice.

Allow the Light of Truth into your spirit and let it overflow for all to see. We must not waiver from Truth when darkness comes to challenge us. When we are brimming with joy and overflowing with the Light of Truth, then darkness looks evermore foolish as it attempts to stand in the Light of Truth and challenge it.

Only fools will align themselves with the darkness when they see it alongside Truth as it foolishly challenges Truth. Truth can never be defeated because it is the only thing that truly exists. Darkness is a fraud that poses as light and vanishes the moment the smallest glimmer of light is seen. The survival of darkness is wholly dependent upon **not** allowing *any* light in. Even the smallest spark of light in your spirit can illuminate the full and straight path to Truth, and then all you need to do is follow that path. Let your cup run over, overflowing with Light and Joy while giving glory to God with your every breath.

Chapter 12

Don't Be Led Astray

We can have our goals firmly set in mind and be walking in the Light of Truth and still be led astray. Evil is always lurking to lead us down a darker path, and those darker paths have varying amounts of light that gradually lead to total darkness.

With each step we take away from our proper and good paths, we see less and less Light and yet we don't notice the changes because they are gradual small increments. As we follow these darkening paths we lose our light little by little, and if we are lucky we will look away from the increasing darkness and realize that we have been led astray and have gotten well off of our proper course. But if we never take the time to look around us because we are so focused on our current trip down those paths leading to darkness, then we will never notice the contrast between where we are now versus from where we have come. Stand strong in your light and always be wary when a path that you are about to step onto is not as well Lighted.

Things Have Been Made Apparent

Life is far more apparent to us all than we allow ourselves to believe. For many of us our troubled paths had all sorts of warning signs that we chose to ignore. We ignored those warning signs because our burning passion for our desires outweighed our commitment to Truth.

When we ignore the many warning signs that stand before us and make the foolish choices that we do, then we are destined to encounter trouble. This problem is very wide-reaching where we are given all sorts of evidence for the best paths, and yet we disregard that evidence on a regular basis because we fail to hear and listen to the whisper of God.

Let's look at Creation as a starting point. Many of us read Genesis chapter one, but we read inadequate translations, thus allowing us to believe erred notions of what actually occurred during the seven steps of Creation. Then, because we read a bad translation we lose faith and we ask "Does God really exist?" We say "show me the evidence" when we have lost all faith and have fallen into darkness.

There's no limit to the evidence of God, but it seems that there is also no limit to our own ignorance. If you read Genesis chapter one and are void of all agenda other than to find the Truth and you use authoritative Bible versions as discussed in *The Science Of God Volume I – The First Four Days*, or *Understanding The Bible* then you will quickly come upon obvious oversights that many people have about what actually occurred during those aspects of Creation.

Everything is there for us to match science and the Bible without fail provided three key points are met. First is by going into it with an open mind. Second, we must understand that theories such as "the big bang" are not really scientifically based and must cheat a great deal to be "proven" because they are merely belief systems. And last, is to reject the six-24-hour-days idea that was indoctrinated in more recent centuries by people who didn't really understand the text or the perspective from which the Creation account was written.

Yes, everything is far more apparent than we would like to admit, but too often man's burning passion to be fools stops us from being able to see through our own darkness.

We Have Been Shown the Way

Much of our folly is inexcusable, yet God does not trample us underfoot. Of course, God has no need to trample us underfoot because we do a great job of that on our own with our own folly.

Our paths have all been made clear and we have been repeatedly told the proper path in the Bible. We also have been told by priests and preachers and family, and most have also told us of the way to salvation. But this book is not about salvation, it is about us being able to show gratitude even when times get tough, along with when times are good.

Pay attention to the signs around you because there are many, and yet we have become too blind to see them. When you're facing troubles, take special care in looking around for the signs that can guide the way down your paths to your good future.

Too often we're all wrapped up in the specific problem at hand and we "can't see the forest through the trees". When we get stuck in our problems in this way, then our focus on the current detail obscures our vision. This is why it's often so easy for someone else to come to us and point out errors that we missed. Due to the fact that they are not trapped in our troubles, they have an advantage to see the whole forest and its problems and potential solutions.

We can also do this for ourselves, but it is certainly more difficult when we're holding onto all of our worries. It is our worries that cause us to have intense focus on one particular detail, thus blinding us from seeing any solutions we might find if we would look at the entire forest. When we place our troubles in the care of God and understand that our inspiration will come, we can then take comfort in that. And if you never noticed this before, now would be an opportune time to take note that the term "inspiration" or "inspire" is derived from the word "spirit". We can think of the word inspiration as in-*spirat*-ion. When we allow the Spirit of Truth to Light our way it is amazing the things we can conceive that are able to lead us out of our turmoil.

When God places the Spirit in us then the solutions begin to become obvious. But we cannot be filled with solutions when we won't release the worries. We have never been instructed to worry, not by Christ and not by God—In fact it is quite the opposite. We are instructed to hand our worries over to God and release them to God so that we can be filled with Truth and solutions that can solve the problems that caused our worry to begin with.

The Revelation

When we release our worries and problems to God, our spirit is freed of the chaos that those problems caused us, allowing us to be filled with ever more Light of Truth, or maybe better understood as *inspired* with Truth or in-*spirit*-ed with Truth. This inspiration has the most amazing power to create all sorts of possible solutions for our many troubles.

We see this in a micro sense when we work on a difficult project and are immersed deeply in it where we cannot seem to make any progress to figure out a way to accomplish some small aspect of the project. But when we leave for lunch and forget about it and we release the problem; then when we return from lunch the inspiration hits us for that "ah-ha!" moment that solves our problem.

God didn't work evermore Creating—After the six critical Creation events God *rested*. This should tell us that *rest* is important to us, especially considering that we are "Created in the image of". The revelations come to us through the Spirit of Truth when we free our minds, hearts, and spirits of needless worries. But, this is not a reason to ignore our problems; in fact it is the exact opposite.

When we have problems and we set our intense focus on some small part of the problem, we end up ignoring the overall problem. Outside input can give us clarity, as well as our handing those worries to God, thus allowing us to be filled with inspiration. It is this inspiration that we are always so excited to tap into, and it becomes all the more common to us when we have handed our troubles to God. We must then give God the praise and thanks that we rightly owe God for allowing us to release those burdens to God.

It is truly amazing how well it works to solve our problems by simply releasing them to the Creator and then stepping away for a bit to refresh our perspective. Often this inspiration comes in short order, allowing us to readily move forward.

Be Careful Who You Follow

When we're trudging through the troubles that life challenges us with, it's easy to grasp at any bit of hope that passes by us. But sometimes that "hope" is not as hopeful as we might think. It's common for people to get themselves involved in bad deals in effort to solve an existing problem. Sometimes this is done through making unwise agreements, and other times it is as simple as following advice of someone who may be sincere, but is utterly wrong for your end goals.

If you have allowed the Truth to be your inspiration, then use that Truth and be extra cautious and diligent when making deals to help you advance to your goals. Also, be extra cautious and diligent in taking advice that is supposed to help you advance. Examine such cases very carefully because often these seemingly attractive lures are just that, they are *lures* that will delay your progress and often will trap you for long periods of time.

We often get so set on accomplishing our goals by a certain date that we take unwise risks that slow us down a great deal. But if we had only been a bit more patient, then another better opportunity would likely have presented itself to us. Some of this might be to test us to see if we are worthy to advance in life, but either way it is just us making bad choices when we follow those who lead us down a wrong path.

The worst thing that we can typically do is the "wrong thing" when it comes to our troubles. Patience is a virtue that has immense value. When we're hurried, we will almost always make mistakes. But when we are patient and pause and allow the inspiration to come to us, then it might take a bit longer to get rolling again, but it is usually far quicker and less expensive to pause and wait rather than to do wrong things. Wrong choices have a tendency to cause more problems than what we started with, and those wrong choices usually cause long delays.

Let Wisdom Be Your Guide

Wisdom is the obvious key to making wise decisions, but wisdom comes from Truth and without the Light that the Spirit of Truth brings we cannot possess wisdom.

Wisdom is our guide that we walk with and the Light of Truth luminates our paths. When our worries are firmly planted in our mind, then the Spirit of Wisdom will be nowhere to be found. We must free ourselves from those burdens and hand them over to God and allow the Light of Truth to inspire us so that wisdom is within our grasp.

We must let wisdom be our guide to all good things. Wisdom allows us to see ahead, unlike worry that clouds our minds. The opposition to *wisdom* is *foolishness*, which includes worry. These two opposed concepts have always been at odds with each other, and worry has been trying to bring us low since the dawn of man.

Doubt is a powerful thing and is what worry is borne of. The Serpent caused Eve to doubt her high position by simply suggesting that she could be like God. This produced in her an immediate feeling of not being good enough which has a great amount of power over us. The sad part is that Adam and Eve were already "Created in the image of", so they already had a God-like nature.

We were Created as perfect beings, clean and free of sin, but when we doubted our position we allowed evil into us, thus darkening our souls. And now we have a very dangerous but satisfying power from the fall of mankind, which is that we now know that we can choose to be guided by the wisdom that is borne of the Light of Truth. Where before the fall in the Garden, we were highly susceptible to evil because we didn't know any better because we simply did not know the difference between what was *good* and what was *evil*. This power of choice in knowing the difference between *good* and *evil* is powerful indeed, and with it we can also destroy ourselves. If we choose wrongly then we must suffer the consequences of our choice of evil. Please choose rightly.

Before the fall of man no one would have suffered any death or hell but because of the fall we are all responsible for our own actions, especially those actions that are harmful to our fellow man. We also have gained the ability to have great wisdom in knowing *good* and *evil*. If we understand the difference between the *good* and *evil* and allow Truth to Light our path, with wisdom as our guide, then we gain a unique ability to see ahead and understand the future consequences that will be caused by what we choose to do in the present. And for this awareness we should be in a state of near constant thanksgiving to the Creator.

Chapter 13

Many Ways

A previous chapter discussed the fact that we have more than one path that we can follow, and many of those paths allow similar outcomes. Some outcomes may be better or worse than others, and some may be indifferent, but all of the *good* paths can lead to your desired outcome.

What we typically don't realize is, though it may appear that there is only one or two paths for us to take, in truth the amount of paths is unlimited to accomplish our goals. Some of those paths obviously make more sense than others and they help to reach the goal faster but could potentially be far more risky than others.

There are many ways to accomplish our goals and we need to pick *one* for specific reasons rather than just randomly picking a direction. After we pick then we should stick with our good pick rather than randomly wandering to and fro between paths. If our selection of one of the many paths is chosen in the absence of wisdom, then it is likely that we will want to change paths several times as we move forward into our future. Find your best path by using the wisdom granted to us by Truth and then plot your course and stand by it. If you run into unexpected troubles, make sure to hand those troubles to God and quiet your mind until the Spirit speaks and you are inspired and can clearly see the way—Patience is critical in that case.

Our Desires Are Like a Vast Pool of Water

We have desires for nearly everything we do, but we don't generally think of our desires specifically as "desires". For instance, if you're thirsty then your desire is going to be for a glass of water or something else to drink. When realizing that we have these seemingly insignificant desires, like a glass of water, it's easy to see that we have a vast pool such desires, but even our greater desires are many. We'll get more into the *importance* of our desires in a later chapter.

The Many People In Our Lives

There is a lot in life where we have *many*. We have many paths to choose from, many desires to pursue, and even many people in our lives. The good people that surround us are true treasures. When we have access to good people we need to be especially grateful to God for those people who are there for us.

Imagine the loneliness we would experience without other people; the only thing worse to us than no people would be only bad people who seek to lead us astray and destroy us.

The value of good people is personally incalculable to us. One very good faithful friend can cheer us up when we're down, and they will stop us from doing stupid things when we have lost sight of our better judgement. One single good friend can be a part of our inspiration and determination; but, we should not be *only* relying on the good assistance and support of our good friends for our success and inspiration. Never forget that our true source on which to depend is the Creator. The Creator will never let us down when our desires are good and help to build up and are in line with the Creator's will.

Having good friends and good people around us is a bonus in life that we must take great care in respecting and in thanking God for. In doing so the value added to the joy of our spirit is greatly increased when good people support our efforts. Doing things all alone and being unable to share those things with others leaves us living a boring lackluster life. It is when we get to share ourselves and what we do or have to offer with friends and family and good people that we get to multiply our joy.

Companionship was amongst the earliest points of Creation that preceded the tangible part of Creation. Then finally man was made in the likeness of God so that the Creator could share all good things with like-minded spirit. This desire to commune and share with others is one of the very important parts of us humans. Most of the time we desire to be around other people who think like us and have desires like us—We are made in God's image.

It's not just those we call "friends and family" who make up the many people around us. There's a world rich with diversity all around us, offering us untold opportunity, experiences, and joy; and all people in this world are a part of the "many people" in our lives.

The Flow of Life

This world and all of Creation have so much to offer all of us. We tend to think that everything is based on our money, but money is only a symbol of our work and it represents the value we assign to it by the agreements that we make for our wage in relation to our time given.

Money flows from person to person as we exchange the value that we personally have assigned to the time that we have given in exchange. Our time flows from one person to another as they buy and use the products or services that we provided. Our time spent is a measure of our existence and that existence flows from one person to another as we materialize it into a service or product. This free-flow of life is what has given us every single man-made product or service ever made.

Without the flow of life, nothing man has ever made would exist and we would all be in it for ourselves never helping anyone and never making anything for others. Each person would have to do everything on their own. Those who have great abilities would have much and those who are "wicked and lazy" would have nothing. This is also true of our culture today as it stands, but because of the flow of life, more people than just the very skilled can exchange their efforts for other good things. Most of us would not be able to do much if everything man-made was suddenly gone. This is because we now have skills that are dependent upon items and ideas that are man-made that exist today.

This wonderful gift of the fluidity of life can be likened to the waters of the oceans and seas. We can all play in them and enjoy them together. And as long as we all play fair and are not harmful to those who we work with, the flow of life will continue increasing for a very long time rewarding us with its benefits for rich and poor alike. We all play in the same pool of life.

Our Unseen Fluidity

What we all miss regarding the flow of life is that each one of us can be overflowing with Truth and goodness, thus giving each of us unlimited potential to do great things. Not things greater than someone else's contributions, but rather just simply other great things. Using our potential ability to flex and flow as we walk down our path makes the trip so much more enjoyable.

When we're rigid like ice we can also be cold like ice, inflexible and susceptible to fracturing and breaking, unable to move effectively. When we allow ourselves to be guided by Truth it's like we are water gracefully flowing down the river's path to our destination. When we choose a wrong path it's more like trying to swim against a torrential current.

We are fluid when we allow ourselves to be so, and this unseen fluidity is very beneficial to us. The rigidity we have is due to our spending too much time in the cold darkness as it freezes our previous flexibility into paths that we believe have only one course of direction. Our inflexible rigidity then leads to ever colder darkness.

Staying free of the bonds of worry and doubt opens our spirit and allows the Light of Truth into us to warm us and keep us fluid so that we can overflow in abundance of Light as we let ourselves flow freely making adjustments in our journey to our good goals. The added inspiration that accompanies *allowing ourselves to use our unseen fluidity* can be very beneficial to us all, for which we must be very thankful.

We Have Many Choices

Life is very much about all of our choices, and there are many choices we can make. Each choice can set off a chain-reaction of other subsequent choices that only we get to make. Each new point of choice is a new path direction. When we allow wisdom to guide us, then each of choice will be more clearly defined in our mind.

Some choices can be mostly indifferent, where others can be distinctly decisive in what will occur next in our lives. Our quest is now and always has been to make the best choices to serve us and those around us so that we can discover and explore and learn more about the Creator in the process.

Our choices will never end, and the more choices we make typically the better we get at making those choices. The gift of choice is beyond measure. Sadly, there are many of us who won't make the required choices, thus causing those choices to eventually be made for us whether we like it or not. Allowing our choices to be decided by luck, chance, or fate will seldom result in an outcome that we truly like. When we fail to make up our minds about life, then we become double-minded, wanting both *this* and *that* when the two ideas are opposed to each other. Such indecisiveness brings mostly strife to you and to those around you. It's much like the parable with the wicked and lazy servant when we fail to use our gift of choice. We can't decide how to move forward to increase our life and the lives of those around us, so we bury that choice and wait to see what happens.

Just as plants need light to thrive, so also our gifted seeds and talents need the Light of Truth to thrive. Begin to exercise your gift of choice, and if you have been lax in doing so then consider making choices and learn quickly from any bad choices, and then move towards the choices that are good.

Nobody gets a pass on this, and making great choices is not a skill we were born with. Most people who make a lot of great choices likely had great examples around them. But what is more common is that they made many bad choices, and over time they learned to differentiate between their good and bad choices, thus allowing them to make mostly good choices later on in life.

Experience is truly the best way to learn, but it can be a most painful time for us. It's interesting to observe the pompous types who when they graduate from college and enter the work force they think they're above it all because they had all sorts of meaningless education. But when it comes to do their actual job they have no idea what to do and must learn most everything through actual on-the-job-training from people with actual experience.

There is nothing that compares to *experience* when it comes to making good and great choices. Over time anyone can learn to make wise choices. And the longer we put off the learning experience of deliberate selection of choice waiting until our hand is forced, then the longer it will take for us to learn to make good choices on our own. In the process we will suffer the unpleasant consequences of allowing this unused gift to sit idle, buried in us until the Master returns. Be grateful for the gift of choice, because with it you can make mostly good choices if you choose to do so, and through those choices you will improve your life and the lives of those around you.

Chapter 14

Life is a Gift

Life is a gift beyond our understanding and its value is very great. Consider why your heart beats—we really don't know why this occurs. We know what happens as it beats and we understand some of how it occurs, but we really don't grasp *why* it actually occurs.

The same is true of most of our key organs. They do amazing things that allow us to live, and there are several of these organs that we cannot live long without. For those who feel that life has cheated them, realize that the "life" that cheats is different from the life that dwells within. Life is a wonderful gift where *we get to choose* whether we will live in joy or in darkness. The intent is for us to choose to live in the Light and fill our lives with gladness and joy and offer our admiration to, and commune with, the Creator. But too often we're all wrapped up in our troubles to a point where we forget to notice the gift that life really is. We also forget what it truly means to us as humans to be able to *talk to our Creator with excitement* just as a child does with a parent.

The Value of Life

What is the value of life? What is the value of **your** life? It's a good bet that your life is worth more than everything you have ever earned or bought all combined throughout your entire life. In fact, I'd be willing to bet that for most people their life is worth more than everything all humans have ever made throughout our entire human history. You might think otherwise, but if you had the total of everything you have ever had or earned all piled up in front of you and you were asked, "Either your life or your things", I feel pretty confident that you would choose your life. Additionally, if you were offered everything that all humans ever made including all money, you would likely do the same. And if you did not, then you're a fool, because if you chose things over your life then you would be too dead to actually enjoy it all. And I doubt that any graveyard would allow it all to be buried along with your dead lifeless carcass.

Our lives mean everything to us, and without our lives we would not **be**. But is life only the beating of our hearts? Is it the world around us that will thrive whether or not we are alive? Is it the things we have built up for years including our money and status? What really is "life"?

In our science labs we are trying to figure out how life began, attempting to create a single living cell that we can call "life", yet we think nothing of ripping an innocent perfectly formed group of cells from the womb of its mother when the mother thinks that her lifestyle is somehow more important than her baby's life. She doesn't want to give up her behavior or the *things* in her life and will instead foolishly give up the life of another *human-being* in exchange for what she wrongly believes is going to amount to more comfort in her life. There is a long-term price to pay for such foolish actions. And the "doctors" who rip innocent children from the wombs of their mothers will also find that there is a heavy long-term price to pay. Yet it's each our own choice to do the foolish things that we each do.

"Life" has a few different meanings, or maybe levels, that include: what we have done all throughout our life, the things we have collected, the beating heart in us along with the breaths we take, and our spirit or soul. Life is also thought of as the cumulative of all of those aspects and more. The physical part of life that's important to us is our beating heart and our breathing because without these functions we'd be dead in short order.

But the most important overall part of life is our *existence*. Without our *spirit existence* we're only an empty vessel that would be less than if we were in a constant coma. Without our spirit we would be only an empty body that would lay there and could never awaken because there is nothing to wake or make alive. Our spirit is the one part of life that we cannot be without because our spirit is **us**. The life of our spirit is the part that we tend to either *fear for*, or to *be excited for*, as we approach physical death.

People try to deny that the spirit exists as an entity unto itself that will live on after our body ends when we have no more breath in us, but this is highly unlikely. Everything we have ever understood in life and our every intuition indicates otherwise. Our conscious will live on whether we like it or not—and our conscious is us. We even go so far as to protect our own conscious and the conscious of those we love, by using violence and death of others when necessary.

Consider situations of war where during battle we will destroy all that we and others have made, to protect what? Is it not the freedom of soul that we so often fight for? Do we not fight to have our *ideals* either advanced or preserved? When we fight in war we are fighting for the freedom of those we love. The one thing that many of us are willing to sacrifice our body for is the lives of those we love, and more importantly for the freedom of choice for the lives of those we love.

When the western world fights wars we are typically fighting for freedom of spirit and life so that our lives may be free to choose Truth. Even though millions have chosen darkness, we still want to allow everyone to *choose* for themselves.

True Life is the conscious that is our spirit—a spirit that is capable of choice. It is *choice* that we hold most sacred, for without it both born and pre-born would not have *free will*.

Life to man is a mix of everything, but the most important part is our soul, mind, essence, spirit, or whatever other description we can come up with. We hold this part of ourself and of others in very high regard, and the value we assign to our spirit truly cannot be numbered.

With all of the methods of government around the world we humans have proven beyond any doubt that *freedom of choice* offers the most robust life with the greatest possibilities. And it is generally only through our free-will choices that we can choose salvation so that we may live in the light of Truth, rather than in eternal darkness.

Life of a Child

In the last section it was mentioned that science is arrogantly attempting to create a living cell and call it "life", while at the same time millions of living cells that a man and woman have created are being torn from the mother and tossed away is if they have no value. We spend billions of dollars every year to try to create "life" in the laboratory and then spend billions to rip perfect living babies from the wombs of their mothers.

It is apparent that our own life, for many of us, is far more valuable than the lives of others. Some people will even kill another human just to steal some meaningless thing they have. But most people value other people's lives as much as and often more than their own life. This is especially true with a decent normal parent, and it seems that the more a parent loves God then the more value they have for their children's lives. There are few parents who would not risk their own life to save their child's life.

We place great value on our own life as well as on the lives of others, especially on our children's lives. Imagine the learning that goes on as the vessel of a child is being filled. When we are young, we can only know what has been set before us. If we are only shown darkness and hatred then that is all we know and thus it is all we are able to offer when we are older. The learning that a child does is hard to measure because of how extensive it is. We often think of learning as the trivia that we learn in school, but the learning that a child does is so much more than what anyone could ever learn in any school even if they spent their entire lifetime in school learning life's trivia.

When does the learning of a child begin? As discussed in the book *Strong Family-A Foundation Of Rock*, the learning of a child truly begins in the womb. When the two living cells from the parents meet, they merge to become one. This single cell then vigorously replicates, with each generation of cells dividing into two new cells. This life continues to thrive in the womb until the fullness of life has fully formed into a perfect child that is ready to enter the world. While the child is in the womb, that child is experiencing a great deal of input such as taste, sounds, and warmth and touch. It is even possible that their smell sense is able to detect odor in the fluid that surrounds them. They might even potentially see faint light if the mother's belly is exposed to bright light. All of these stimuli cause the child to move around in the mother's womb letting the mother know that all is well. This life that has formed inside of the mother has great value to the mother, and good mothers will instinctively protect the life of the child in any way they can. We all owe a great deal of gratitude to and for the mothers who carried us in them for the better part of a year, and we owe great thanks to God that they had a profound instinct to protect us.

An Active Mind is an Active Soul

If your mind is not doing anything then your soul is likely dead. It is not possible for us to not be thinking about something. Even if we try to imagine that we are not thinking about anything then we are probably thinking about not thinking about anything. Our active mind is a wonderful gift that we can use as we each choose to use it.

If we choose to use our mind to entertain darkness then darkness will be our home, but if we choose to use our mind to entertain light then light will be our home. Our *thoughts* are the precursor to what we will say and do, and what we say and do is a reflection of what we have *thought* or are currently *thinking*, allowing others to grasp what is in our mind.

Consider how difficult it must have been for God to come to the realization of *communication* and then to go on to imagine a way to actually cause others to be Created. The Creator's mind must be an extremely active mind, ever thinking about Creating and companionship, and then devising a means by which other souls can come into existence and communicate with God. It is truly awe inspiring!

We humans, who are Created in-the-image-of, also have active minds that don't stop. If our mind was ever able to completely stop then it is entirely possible that we would not exist. Or at least we would not exist to others and would likely be caught in eternal solitude because we would be cut off from all other spirit.

Our active minds are our only notification that we actually exist. The very fact that we can *think* is our essence and without it what would we really be? Our inquisitive nature causes us to *question* things and then search for the answers to those questions. There is a great deal of power for us in "*I wonder*". It is the *wonder* within us that makes us natural explorers whether young or old.

The ability to wonder is what solves all of our problems. Wonder gets us in trouble at times when we're not careful, but it's the most wonderful gift to be thankful for nonetheless.

Sometimes It's Just Great to Be Alive

Did you ever have one of those days where everything is right and you feel that it's just great to be alive? Most of us have had these days. Often this feeling is evoked when we have everything in order and the weather conditions that are favorable to us happen to be present at that same time—Ah... If only life could always be this way.

But if life was always this way then we likely wouldn't even really ever appreciate it because we would be so accustomed to it that we wouldn't even notice it. It's interesting how we can get so accustomed to something special to a point that it no longer feels special to us. This is like snacks and treats that once upon-a-time were rare, but now have become so common that many of us have them regularly as if they are meals, and for our lack of realization we pay for it at the waistline. Or maybe we struggled to finally reach our goal and we now finally have that home that we were so excited to get, but now that we have it we have grown so used to it that we actually complain about it because we must maintain it. Yet when we first bought it we were so excited even to do the maintenance.

Sometimes we need to step back from our current situation just for the purpose of appreciating what we actually do have. Let's say that you have a car that has lots of broken things but it still works and you currently cannot afford a different one. Ask yourself next time you complain about this car, "would I rather drive it, or *walk* to work in the dead of winter?"–and suddenly that car becomes a luxury!

Much of the toil we feel that we have in life is really an issue of *perspective*. This is not suggesting that we should forfeit our desires for such things like a new car, but we can certainly realize that we should appreciate what we currently have and the luxury and value that such things bring to us. If you have any doubts about this then try to not use any of these seemingly insignificant things. You would quickly learn to appreciate something as simple as a light switch if it was somehow gone the next time you reached to turn the lights on at night.

Take time to stop yourself and take note of all of the tiny little luxuries that we have in life and take the time to realize that it's just great to be alive! Then realize that eventually the tough times will pass provided that we start making wise choices now. Give thanks to God for every small thing in your life–It's much more difficult to have a bowl of cereal in the morning if you don't have a bowl. We all can be very thankful for something as simple as fire that generates the electricity we use for most everything we do. Yes, sometimes it's just great to be alive!

How Life is Meant to Be Lived

It's just great to be alive!—*That* is how life is meant to be lived. We humans were Created free of all burdens and troubles and had only one task–to care for the Garden. We were intended to care for things, discover things, and learn things; *Toil* was never in the original intent. It is our human affinity towards greed and corruption that causes almost all of our troubles in this world.

Imagine for a moment if you had no troubles, no debt, and no other contractual obligations–your life would be very carefree! Don't think for a moment that the Creator wanted us to suffer the many troubles that we suffer today. Very few of our troubles are caused by nature, because most troubles are of our own making.

We didn't have to take that particular job, or sign for that particular loan, or use as much electricity or heat as we did, or even build our house on the ocean's shore. We can drive a smaller or older car, and we can live in a less expensive home, and we can take responsibility and properly discipline our children. There is almost no problem that we did not create on our own. Even when someone else is the root of our problems, we still typically have the power to separate from such troublesome people.

If we ever want to live life as it was meant to be lived, we first must realize that we are meant for joy and we are built for joy. When we're joyful then our bodies produce chemistry that is good for the body, but when we worry or are stressed then the body produces bad chemistry that over long periods can be very harmful to us. If this is not indicative of how we are supposed to live, then what evidence can persuade someone that we are truly built for joy?

Our design is very obvious when you understand that it is an actual *design*. When we choose to doubt that we have been Created, then we lose the notion of *design* because design is specifically a Creative action, and creating can only be done through discernment. Discernment is an action that requires mind and spirit and thinking and reason. We can duplicate some of these things with computers, but then we must realize that the computers were also *designed*. If we evolved, then we truly have no more worth than an ant or a tree or a slug or even a rock. But somehow we understand that man's value is far greater than all other things, living or inanimate.

It's ironic how some of us will demand evidence that we were Created rather than having had evolved, yet there is little or no evidence that man evolved from some primordial soup. Most representations of the "missing links" found to our supposed evolution are fraudulent, which can be easily witnessed by taking the time to study the findings. In doing so you will discover that these findings are mostly guesswork. The majority of the most critical skeletons are nothing more than creative guesswork done by artists who fashion the missing parts to look as the artists are paid to make them look.

The truth is that most evidence points to us having been uniquely Created with specific design. Our very specific design has many attributes pointing to our purpose. First we have our input devices, such as ears to hear with, our hands to touch and work with, our eyes to see with, our mouths to speak kindness and love or even taste with, and a nose to smell with. These input devices clearly indicate that we are meant to receive and explore. Next, we have a unique mind that has a strong ability to love and care for other people and care for creation. The mind of man also has an ability to *wonder* beyond what any other known creature does. This is also indicative of our purpose to explore. Add to this the previously mentioned body chemistry that is favorable to us when we are in a state of joy, then you should get very a clear understanding our intended purpose.

When you add up the obvious indicators in our design, we are clearly designed to be carefree and loving and inquisitive and to explore. This means that we are to be like children are while they play. They discover, explore, love, and are very joyfully carefree! That is how life is meant to be lived, and for this we must give thanks to God and show our everlasting gratitude by living our *purpose*.

Chapter 15

We Can Agree

Oh the troubles we cause with all of our disagreements. We disagree about politics, we disagree about religion, we disagree about raising a family, we disagree about business, we disagree about love, and we disagree about most things at some point. A lot of our disagreement has to do with our chosen paths. When we choose paths that are not in alignment with what is good and true then we can arrive at nearly any thought or opinion no matter how irrational, even if it will ultimately harm us.

When we're not following the Light of Truth, then our thoughts and paths can be irrationally unlimited. In our unlimited irrationality we still have a creative ability to dream up just about any irrationality having benefit to only ourselves with little or no benefit to others, and actually often being a detriment to others. Most disagreements with others, or even with God, are grown from our irrationality and self-serving greed.

Life could be very good and very agreeable if only we would find it in ourselves to see things through the eyes of others and consider *their* concerns and troubles. One of the parts of life that is most troubling to us is when we have disagreements in situations involving love. This can be with any person who we hold as dear, such as family. But mostly we feel the greatest pain in close intimate relationships of man and woman who are dating or married.

We invest a great deal of our love and deeply expose ourselves to the person who we chose to offer access closest to the heart, but when that access is violated then comes the pain. This will happen to some extent in almost all relationships, but it gets real bad real fast when we refuse to *consider each other's deepest feelings*. Sometimes this is done in a sort of oblivious state with the person not realizing it, but it is no less painful for the recipient of that oblivion. More often it is just the selfish nature of us that causes us to not consider how the other person feels. *Red Hot Marriage-The Marriage Manual* explores this and many other points, but the starting point is to see life through the eyes of others.

We truly do have the ability to live in a world without this sort of strife, and when we choose a more agreeable path we then will always find life to be far more pleasant. The problem is that we ourselves can decide to be more considerate, but if the other person or people who we are dealing with will not be more considerate, then it still presents problems to us. It is our selfish and very persistent nature of *what's-in-it-for-me* that causes almost all of our problems. For instance, you could be in a dating or marriage relationship and be thinking you just want to be left alone, but the other person wants to be with you. Who is in the wrong in that case? It could be both or it could be one or the other because it is going to all depend upon how much balance is found in the relationship. Yet the whole point in such relationships is to be together, so if a person is insistent on *always* being alone, then it's unfair to the other person who wants to be with their love interest. If the person had known that their companionship would ever have been *unwanted* then they would likely not have entered the relationship to begin with.

Every situation ranging from business to marriage shares the same problem of *selfishness* when there is a breakdown in the relationship. Somewhere someone is doing, or not doing, something that the other person or people expected. It doesn't matter if the expectation is reasonable or not because the troubles begin with the differing perspectives of the situation and its expectations.

We can all agree on most everything when we use the Light of Truth as our guide and stay clear of those who do not know the Light. But when we engage in agreements with people who we know are not being fair and are being irrational, we have then chosen a foolish path. Yes, we *can* all agree if only we would put away our selfish nature of taking more than we deserve and are willing to work for.

It is when both parties in any type of agreement are fully considerate of the other party in the agreement that it can be a joyful agreement for all involved. This is when marriages and business agreements alike will flourish and everyone can benefit. Any agreement of any sort will do the same when we chose to rationalize our thoughts through the Light of Truth. Our agreements to God are no different, and we all must understand that whether we exist or not, the Creator will always exist and our "agreements" with the Creator are usually *our own* promises that we made that are typically not kept by us. Most of us violate our agreements with God at least to some extent. We can all agree that we are blessed just to be alive when we consider how inconsiderate most or all of us are in regard to our agreements with God. Let us all thank God that God is *very* patient with us.

Your Foundation

To live a joy-filled life, even during times of trouble, there's nothing more important than a solid foundation. Sure, we can build on higher ground and even solidly attach ourselves to that ground. But if the foundation on which we build is not solid then we will be swept away in our river of troubles. When it really comes down to it, there are very few of us that have the proper foundation of the unmovable rock that we need, and if we have happened to stumble upon it then it typically slips from our grasp because we have failed to *attach* ourselves to it. There are three key points to consider regarding our foundation: The first, of course, is to find the high ground. Next is to make sure that it is a foundation of rock. And finally, we must attach ourselves to it so that we cannot be swept away during the floods of adversity. Without these three points we are sure to encounter countless troubles and we will feel the pain as we struggle through them.

To attach ourselves we must embrace and hold dear the Light of Truth shown to us by The Christ, and when we have found the Light then we have found the higher ground that is made of rock. This is the "enlightenment" that so many people talk about, but most fail to receive. The Light of Truth has no price because a price cannot be placed on the ultimate in existence. But this does not mean that you or I cannot afford it. The Light of Truth is free for all who choose to embrace it.

There are two types of foundation: One is the ground that we choose to build our lives upon, and the other is the foundation that we ourselves lay for our lives. We can find and attach ourselves by embracing the Light of Truth, but then too often we attempt to bury it with our irrational foundations which will slip right off of the rock of Truth the moment it begins to rain.

That Which Supports Us

The foundation that supports us is the Light or Darkness that we choose to build our lives upon. When we choose the darkness then we will always be groping around in the dark trying to find our way, and that is why so many of us have so many troubles. That which supports us guides us. When we have chosen darkness as our support, it guides us to error and indecision causing us untold troubles.

When we choose the Light of Truth of God, then we have a much easier time in life and can avoid the countless struggles that would otherwise stand before us blocking our way. We need to be thankful that God will guide our way and support our endeavors when we are on the right path, yet we still have to realize that darkness will try to stop all good things. However, when we choose to follow the Light of the Creator we are then emotionally prepared for such setbacks and can more readily overcome them. When we embrace the Light we know that setbacks will arise. But through the wisdom that is provided by the Light that we have embraced, we become more able to recognize such setbacks far earlier and defeat them far more quickly.

Individual Support

Support from people around us is also important to us. When we choose a path that is a bit more challenging, it's also more challenging to find people who can find it in themselves to support us in our challenging endeavors. Just finding people *who will not discourage* our efforts is in itself is sometimes a difficult task, let alone having them *actually support* our endeavors.

Those who are remote from our problems will often discourage us, saying things like "When are you going to give up and get a job?" or "Get a different job." These are certainly *not* points of encouragement and they are often very discouraging to us. There is great value in other people *not* discouraging us, yet even their discouragement can be of value to us when we use it wisely.

It's common for others to render an opinion about our personal situation. When we use negative opinions as a sort of check-system to validate our own ideas, then their negativity can be used for our own good. Sometimes that negativity is correct because we might be about to turn down a wrong path, and when we use their negativity as a springboard to analyze our intentions, we can then see whether or not their points are valid. This check-system helps us to be sure that we are making right choices. Use this to your advantage, because if you can't overcome other people's negativity, then it is possible that they're right. Also, if you're not willing to overcome *inaccurate* negativity, then do you really deserve to succeed in your endeavors?

People who blindly support us are often invaluable to us and should be cherished by us, but if they are not actually processing our situation or plans then they can become a snare to us in that they become a false sense of security. Where on the other hand, opposition is often painful to us, but forces us to think very carefully as to whether or not we are making the right choices. Having only "yes-men" around us is dangerous. There's a difference between individual support, and the dangers of a "yes-man" who will always tell you that your ideas are great even when those ideas are not great.

People who offer support that is of high quality will engage their mind, causing them to ask you questions as they process the things you're discussing with them. They are neither negative nor a "yes-man". They have true interest in you and in your life and will help you think through your troubles and difficult situations and perplexing challenges even if they don't fully grasp them. Just the verbal and mental engagement that they offer you is invaluable to you in that it allows you to talk and think things through audibly with them, but more importantly with yourself after you speak with them.

Sometimes we talk to ourselves to help ourselves to think things through, but the individual support of others can truly increase the value of talking and thinking through our problems. Make sure to thank your friends and family who are willing to do this with you. And always remember that God is also always there for us to do the very same. We need to be thankful to God for such individual support.

The Gift of Like Minds

Individual support is great and is truly a gift, but a *like-mind* is on a completely different level. Having a *like-mind* to consult with has unparalleled value, and only quieting our minds and listening to the whisper of the Creator exceeds it.

A *like-mind* is not a "yes-man" who will agree with everything we say or think, nor it is a negative person who will denounce everything we say or think. A *like-mind* is good individual support, but is on a whole new level. A like-mind will share the pains and hurts with you. Even if they are not responsible for any of it, they will still feel your hurts and joys and share the disappointments and excitement with you. They will speak up when they see you making a foolish mistake, and they will support you when they see you making wise choices. Sometimes a like-mind will be a business partner, or maybe a spouse, and is directly involved with the tasks at hand. But often the person is just a great person who takes real interest in what you're working on, or they take interest in helping to solve the troubles you face. They offer sound thoughts with possible solutions or paths that you might take, and they will analyze those paths with real connection and understanding.

The gift of a like-mind is truly priceless. People who stop and hear and listen to what you're talking about and fully consider the situation that you're facing, whether good or bad, will understand the needs of the situation and that can help you a great deal. Often these people are experienced and they love to help. When they're experienced and are familiar with the sort of situation that you're working through, then they are usually full of much wisdom and know and understand the pitfalls and the advantages of the various paths you might take.

It's easy to get caught up in thinking that like-minded people are truly a gift and are *only* helpful when we're working on our problems or troubles. But don't forget that even when everything is going along fine, receiving added wisdom can make "going along fine" turn into going along fantastic! Cherish these people, for they are a true gift to have in your life. Always thank them for their help, and thank God for them.

One single word from a person of wisdom at the right time can make more difference than most of us can ever imagine. There can be thousands of potential solutions for any one problem, and some of those solutions might be out of our grasp, yet other solutions are close at hand yet we simply never even conceive them as a possibility, and thus they fall completely out of our consideration. But one word from the right person at the right time can connect us with the right people or inspire us to think the right thought that will quickly allow us to proceed in confidence of success. Yes, these experienced people of like-mind are a true gift from God to be very thankful for.

We Can Bear It

When we have great people around us it's wonderful and is of great assistance in life and for our staying in joy. But as mentioned in an earlier chapter, it's not a good idea to depend only on these people because they might have their own problems to deal with. If we are dependent upon them and their moral support, then if they're having a bad day or are not available, we tend get stuck and cannot advance without them. This is often referred to as being "co-dependent" and it is a slippery slope to be trapped on.

We should all work towards being able to bear the good times and the bad times on our own. But this does not mean that we should push others away and do everything alone. It means that our joy and forward progress should not be solely dependent on other people. We can depend on the Creator in this way, but the work is still incumbent upon each of us to do on our own. The Creator gets little from our advancing unless we are bringing more people towards salvation. Our work is generally for our own joy and for the joy of those immediately around us—It is *our* work and *our* own responsibility.

If we can engage other people to lend a hand or an ear to us, then we must count that as a blessing and as a bonus. As adults we each are no one else's responsibility but our own. Always prepare yourself to bear it all alone and rejoice when someone is willing to bear it with you! Thank them, and then also thank God for the assistance of good people.

Chapter 16

Seeing Through It All

Oh the clutter we saddle ourselves with. It seems safe to say that most of us who have had times of struggle can look back and pick out many things that we would now do differently if faced with the same situations again. This is *wisdom* at work, allowing you to foresee the future and enabling you to determine what will occur when certain actions are taken by you. Because you have experienced certain things, you are now capable of determining the consequence of a given action within a given circumstance. But when we're on round-one of life, it's very difficult to see all of the pitfalls that we might encounter.

Life has much to offer with unlimited choices, which all becomes a bit cloudy when we are in the midst of a new or troubling venture in life. When our inexperienced eyes look forward, we simply cannot fathom all that can go wrong, thus we generally are incapable of seeing through it all. For many of us, if we had known the troubles we would encounter we probably would have never made the attempt to begin with. All of the unseen details quickly become a dense fog to us thus obscuring the best path for us to take. This is usually when we begin to panic and do the wrong things.

The painful experiences that the experienced people endured are their gold, and many of those people are willing to freely give some of that gold to us if we promise to pass it forward when our time comes to help those who follow us. Once you have gone through the fire, you begin to have a clarity of vision that is tough to match through any other means. This clarity of vision can help in most parts of life, if not *all* parts of life. This clarity is the general wisdom that comes with age and truth simply because we have accumulated more life experiences.

We Can See

Our experiences all come through our input devices, one of which is our eyes. The gift of sight is one of those many things that we take for granted, but anyone who has lost their vision now knows better. Just stop to think what it would be like to see *nothing* and still have to navigate through life. I recommend against actually trying to navigate through life with our eyes closed, but just imagine having to walk through an unfamiliar store without the gift of sight. Just trying to think through such a scenario causes us to really appreciate the struggles blind or severely visually impaired people deal with every day.

If we lay down at night in the dark with curtains drawn and shades pulled with our eyes closed to get the best sense of blindness, and then imagine walking around in a store, or down a sidewalk in the city and trying to cross traffic, we still see the picture in our mind. Even if we try to imagine being blind we really cannot do it because we have seen. The mind sees as clearly as do our eyes when it comes to our vision. In fact, most of us probably navigate our house in the middle of the night in near total darkness as we make our way to the bathroom for an occasional midnight visit. When we do so, we are unconsciously picturing the path as we make our way. The only time this is ever a problem is when we or someone else left something we did not expect in that path, causing us to stumble.

Consider the ease with which we navigate life because of our eyes: We don't just use them to navigate life going from here to there, life navigation includes things like reading, and watching general and educational entertainment. We can look up at the sky and realize that it might soon rain, allowing us to quickly do some important outdoor task before the rain arrives. There are so many seemingly insignificant things that our vision assists with that we simply do not realize. Try keeping your vision in mind for an entire day as you navigate your day, whether it's physical here-to-there navigation or something as simple as looking at the price tag on something at the store, or the changing of the stop light at the intersection. You will quickly be amazed and grateful for the gift of vision and all that it does for you. Doing so should give you renewed respect for anyone who struggles due to impaired vision, especially those who are completely blind.

Our ability to see is a wonderful gift and we should give thanks for all of the beauty that we can take in every single time we open our eyes.

We Can Hear

We think that eyesight is the beat-all of the senses, but let us not think any less of our hearing. Hearing is a most wonderful sense that we have. This input device allows us to do simple things such as enjoy music or hear the voice of a cherished loved one. We can hear danger approaching and sense approximate distance of a noise. We can tell if someone is near to us or far from us without seeing them. We can typically determine if we are indoors or outside just by the sounds that we hear. Our hearing works much like a radar or sonar allowing us to sense objects. We might not get a great amount of detail about a specific object, but often we can tell that something is there just by being familiar with an area and hearing certain expected reflected sounds when those echoes come back to our ears.

Proximity and direction are only a small part of what our hearing can do for us. Just consider for a moment exactly what is occurring when you "hear" something. When we hear, our eardrum vibrates, and then those vibrations wiggle a tiny bone and some hair-like structures that somehow send signals to our brain. Our brain then processes those signals and renders them as sound to our mind. Our mind interprets what we have just heard and allows us to respond in voice, action, or thought. This in itself is amazing, but it is the *understanding* of what we have heard that is truly amazing.

The gift of hearing, like sight, is one of those things that we don't want to be without, and if you were to be without it you would quickly have compassion for those who cannot hear at all. However, in our modern culture we do have some familiarity with being deaf in a slightly different way. As just described, our hearing allows us to sense proximity or distance and direction without us really even specifically noticing it. It's difficult to explain the many ways in which this keeps us safe, but in our modern world many of us go through part of the day with headphones on or "ear buds" in our ears listening to music— sometimes with tragic consequences. It's not necessarily that we're distracted by this, though that's often true, rather the sound is often played at so great a volume so as to overpower the sounds of our immediate environment, thus causing us to not be able to hear an approaching car or other such danger. Having our sonar abilities being blocked by loud music has caused many injuries and deaths over the years due to people walking into traffic or doing some other dangerous or deadly action. These dangers would have been otherwise avoided had their hearing been tuned into the environment rather than to the loud music.

In the situation where our music overrides the sound of the immediate environment, we put ourselves at unnecessary risk and are at a greater disadvantage than even a completely deaf person is. This is because we still have our hearing and we expect that we will somehow be audibly warned and able to anticipate those sounds to notify us to proceed with caution. The loud music blocks our ability to be warned, but a completely deaf person, on the other hand, does not have the feeling of security that the rest of us take for granted. The deaf have their other senses more finely tuned to the immediate environment in order to receive their notifications of danger to keep them safe. We can safely assume that many of those who have been injured due to such audible catastrophes probably now realize that hearing their immediate environment is very important to their own well-being.

But our hearing doesn't stop at our physical environment; it also includes our personal relationship environment. Many of us have people in our lives that are important to us, such as a spouse or child, or a girlfriend or boyfriend. We hear these people, but while at times we completely take them for granted, most of us would be broken-hearted if we could not hear their voices. Our hearing allows us to care for young children without having to have them in plain view at every waking moment. And in a bit of irony with young children, as most any parent knows, it is often when we *can't* hear them that we know that they are causing a bit of mischief.

We Can Listen

Our ability to *hear* is one thing, but without *listening* our hearing is really quite useless. Take for example the care of a child and *not* hearing the little one. When this occurs, a parent hears that there is a noticeable silence rather than normal child-at-play noises coming from the next room. It is our listening process that allows us to consider this noticeable silence and understand it as the child, in their innocence, being deeply occupied in something that they probably should not be doing.

The sounds of a child at play have recognizable sounds such as the clacking sound of their blocks as they build and knock down their creations. When we set them in a safe environment and give them toys to play with and discover, we then unconsciously expect certain sounds to emanate from that room. When the room is silent we know that they are no longer playing with their blocks.

But listening for a child at play is just one small part of our ability to listen. Listening is our ability to process what we have heard, and that ability typically gets better as we age. If you ever had a heated discussion with someone, you might recall you or the other person saying something like "why won't you *listen* to me?", they know that you heard them because you were right next to them and they were speaking plenty loud. But they asked if you were "listening". *Listening* is us *processing* the things that we hear and then responding appropriately.

As your listening gets better with age, you will likely recall life and remember things that your parents told you, and you will likely remember an ah-ha moment when their seemingly empty words suddenly came to life as you experienced what they spoke of or warned you to be alert for. Your heard them back then, but only truly listened when you had your ah-ha moment.

Listening is also a truly great gift and it is not just with our ears that we listen. Listening occurs through all of our senses. If you step outside and feel the cold air, you process that input and realize that you must put on a heavier jacket in order to keep warm or you might freeze to death. If you see rain clouds on the horizon that are headed your way you might choose to grab a raincoat. If you hear a car coming down the street you will wait for it to pass before you cross the street. If you smell unexpected smoke you will check for unwanted smoke or fire. If you begin to eat something and it tastes spoiled you will spit it out and rinse your mouth out. All of our senses can be listened to by us and it is our *listening ability* that allows us to respond accordingly.

In all cases just mentioned where we listen to our senses to avoid danger, we must also consider that we listen to our senses for good things too. For instance, when we smell the smell of warm cookies in the oven or fresh baked bread we can tell that they are almost ready to be served. Your love-interest can whisper some sweet-nothings in your ear to which you can respond in the desired manner. You can feel the warmth of the house as you step inside on a blustery winter day. You can see a work of art, whether it be a person's work or an actual person you love. And you can taste the freshly baked cookies or bread as you eat what you previously could smell when it was ready to come out of the oven.

You can see as you have listened to these words that *listening* is very different from *hearing* and it is *listening* that makes life so very enjoyable. **Listen** to others. Always be Grateful for your ability to *listen*, because without it we would only have the capacity of animals—if we were lucky.

We Can Know

Knowing things comes along with listening. When we *know* something, we have listened to the situation with all of our senses and made conclusions based upon that which came through our senses. For instance, if you reach out and touch a wall that you see and feel, and also hear with your sonar hearing, you will have a pretty clear understanding that the wall exists and therefore you know that it is there. You will then know to not attempt to walk through the wall because you know from experience that walls are not intended to walk through, and such an attempt could be very painful for you.

Knowing something is always based up our sensory input, and we hear that input and make analysis of the input by listening to it. But "knowing" something is sometimes not particularly accurate. This is because we can choose to ignore some of the input. Doing so allows us to draw inaccurate conclusions. Take for example someone who has chosen to "know" that "there is no God." Against all evidence, someone makes such a statement because they have chosen to ignore the vast mountains of evidence. By ignoring the evidence taken in by the senses they can claim to "know" something to be true even though they are completely incorrect.

"Knowing" without full understanding and consideration crosses the line from ignorance to foolishness. This is where the Light of Truth comes in. When you have The Light of Truth in you then you will refuse to ignore additional information pertaining to the knowledge you seek.

We Can Understand

Understanding is more than just "knowing". Understanding goes far beyond *knowing* and takes into full consideration all of the sensory input that we receive. *Understanding* is then processed through the filter of the Light of Truth and we can come to reasonably safe conclusions and know something with reserve. True understanding will always remain open to new evidence of other possibilities but will be reserved and not suddenly jump to new conclusions. True understanding is passionate about understanding and cares nothing of the *appearance* of being "right". Understanding is about being *accurate* in our assessments of any given situation.

When we understand, we can then know things that we would otherwise generally guess at. This can be scientific issues, like the questions surrounding Creation and whether or not it was done as a sort of spontaneous self-ignited explosion, or if it was more gently done as an active action by a discerning Creator as discussed in *The Science of God.* We can also understand simple things such as the dangers of not paying close attention to our immediate environment. When we understand that our senses are notifying us of dangers, it is through our past experiences and ability to forecast danger that we know through our understanding something will hurt us if we are not cautious when in close proximity to it.

Then we have perhaps the most important part of understanding which is that of our personal relationships. Our relationships are a bit more complex than are issues of science and danger. This is because relationships have the added complexity of our personal feelings where both we and those whom we communicate with have personal feelings about the things we *believe* we "know". As we tread the paths of our personal relationships, we can take comfort in our understanding of not only the facts of a given situation, but also of our understanding of the person that we are with. If we know and understand that the other person we are talking with is an irrational person, then we have the ability guide the conversation to a more pleasant outcome than we would otherwise be able to. Sometimes it's ourself who is the irrational person.

Whether or not the other person is irrational, we also have the ability to be compassionate and loving, while also understanding that someone might be feeling pain about a particular situation. Our ability to show compassion is typically greatly appreciated by those who are in some sort of suffrage. We can also understand *love* when someone has a deep interest in us and us in them, where we are able to exchange that love in deep and meaningful ways.

Without *understanding* we lose all of our human in-the-image-of-God-like qualities. Let's be ever thankful for being "made in the image of" with an ability to understand. We can talk to animals, but they will only look back with no ability to understand in the same way or at a level that man does. This speaks for the unique nature of our Creation for which we must all be eternally grateful.

Chapter 17

Share Your Experience

A big part of our gratitude is when we share it. If we are very thankful in mind only, then those who we are grateful to, or for, will not have any indication that we even care about them or what they may have done for us. But when we share our internal gratitude it allows those to whom we are grateful to receive that gratitude. I once heard a story about someone who wrote a thank-you letter to a grandparent and it was relayed that the thank-you was truly felt as a gift by the grandparent who then joyfully shared this experience with friends. This example helps us to understand how important it is to tell others that we are grateful for what they have done, or even just for them being in our lives.

If you think about your life, you can probably recall a time in your life where someone didn't thank you for what you had done for them. Their ingratitude was probably somewhat insulting since you went out of your way to help them. And truth be told, we ourselves have likely done the same to others.

We must take care in sharing our gratitude with those to whom it is owed—Thinking it is not enough. When we offer assistance to someone and they ungratefully take it for granted, it typically reduces our desire to offer them assistance in the future. If we did choose to help in the future, then the subsequent unappreciated assistance we give becomes ever more difficult for us to offer. This is problematic in friendships, and even more so in a marriages.

When we are thanked with *authentic* gratitude it has a tendency to cause us to want to do more in the future, should the need arise. This isn't just true with us and other people; it's also true with us and God. If we have an attitude of **in**gratitude then can we really expect that the Creator is going to want to do more for us? It's highly unlikely that such an attitude will benefit us in any way. But when we offer *sincere* thanks in our subsequent prayers then we're more likely to be listened to.

Telling and Explaining Are Two Different Things

Just telling someone "thanks" is good and is as it should be, but only telling falls short of true gratitude. Think of this in relation to teaching a child to be thankful to friends and family when they receive gifts from them. The child will get the gift and be immediately and completely enthralled with the gift not realizing that they owe a bit of thanks to the person who gave them the gift. Then as is typical, the parent of the child will tell the child to say thank you, at which time the child will offer the thanks but still not really be in a truly thankful mindset due to their preoccupation with the gift. This sort of acknowledgement is truly important in marriages.

It's not that they are specifically not thankful; it's just that the thanks is far from their mind, if realized at all. However, if that child were to open the gift and look at the giver with a look of complete appreciation and with no one telling them to "say, thank you", then when the words come out of their mouth it will have much more meaning to the giver of the gift.

It is when our senses have received and we have listened to the offering by others *and then processed and understood* the given offering we just received, that we can truly offer <u>authentic</u> gratitude.

Telling is sort of like hearing in that it's a function that does not necessarily require understanding, just like hearing doesn't require listening. *Telling* is only saying words, but *explaining* requires understanding, at least to some extent it does. Without us understanding that which we feel that we are "explaining", we are merely talking and repeating things that other people have said or written. We see a great deal of this in the system of "higher education". College is intended to be a place for people to learn in attempt to become enlightened, but all too often it's a place to learn needless trivia. Some college professors do nothing more than repeat what they believe they have learned from their own college professors when they attended school.

We can have all of the education offered in the world, but if we fail to filter it through the Light of Truth and accurately understand it, then we are among those who are wrong. This is because then we merely repeat incorrect things that other people have said—Things which can be either right, or entirely wrong and incorrect.

It is only when we truly understand something that we can fully explain it to others. When they ask questions, we should have well thought-out answers in reply, or at least say that we are unsure or do not know the answer to their question. When we "*tell*" we are only repeating or saying what we are supposed to say. When we *explain with understanding* then it is usually very apparent in our words, emotions, and general demeanor that we have deep understanding of what we are explaining.

When we give thanks, especially to God, it's good if we are able to explain what we are thankful for and how it made us feel.

We need not go into deep detail, but showing *authentic* gratitude to our fellow man or to God has great value. The authenticity comes from the understanding that is gained by processing the input through listening through the Light of Truth. Make sure that when you show gratitude it is authentic!

Are We Bragging?

When great things happen to us and we share those things, sometimes people will take it as us bragging, but such a perspective is often due to their misunderstanding. When people "brag", it is usually due to their feelings of inadequacy. Those who feel inadequate also see other people's sharing of good news as the same as when they themselves brag in effort to fraudulently inflate themselves so that they feel as if they have worth equal to or above others.

When sharing news of our accomplishments or of gifts we have received then we have a right to share that good news, and sometimes it's almost a duty to do so. If God grants us success or protection, then isn't it worthy of "bragging" about that gift and about God's greatness? We should do so in order to spread the word and tell the world how wonderful God is when we receive the promises that God made to us all.

Surely we should share our good news at appropriate times and in appropriate situations, because there are times when our good news could either help or hurt someone. If a person has just received very bad news, then our good news can make them feel worse; so at times it's best to hold our tongue and feel their sorrow with them. But in many cases our good news can be an inspiration to those who are feeling down.

After we consider the circumstances, then at some point there is an appropriate time to brag on God and all that God has done in our lives. While shouting from your rooftop may be a bit dangerous, especially if you live in a two-story house, we can certainly share our joy as we proceed through our days when the situation is appropriate. Let us all tell the world of the Greatness of God—our Creator.

Make Sure to Tell God

With all of our excitement and hurrying about when good things come our way, let us not forget, as young children typically forget, to offer our gratitude to God for all of the good things that God has done for us, and for all of the small things that make us able to enjoy the good things that God does for us. Without our senses and without our ability to discern and understand, we become unable to enjoy anything. Tell God how grateful you are for all of the wonderful things in your life that enable you to enjoy life, and also for those things that allow you to overcome adversity. And thank God for the ability to overcome adversity and for the ability to learn from it so that you can work to avoid similar adversity in the future.

With Full Expression and Passion

When you give thanks to someone, do so with expression and passion. There is no need to go overboard and fake being passionate and excited about something someone has done if you really don't feel excited. But there is also no reason to hide your excitement when you're grateful for them or for something that they did for you or for others.

All too often we, in our reserved adult way, will hide our true emotions for fear of being "too excited". But if that excitement is authentic, then don't be so sure that you are being "too" excited. Our passionate and excited moments of life are often our best and are when we are at our best. Withholding this joy just to be seen as a "cool-kid" is foolish. We might keep our excitement at a level that fits the environment, but to withhold it altogether is actually somewhat insulting to those who contributed to that excitement.

If God has given you good health and yet times are tough, but you have moments of realization of your good health and how wonderful it is to have it, then express those realizations to God with thanks and praise. When you're sick in bed suffering from a terrible cold that you caught at work, realize the glorious comfort of being able to be in a warm bed as you care for yourself in effort to get better. Express your passion that the warm comfortable bed evokes when you realize how fortunate you are to be able to be there, rather than being out in a cold and wet environment that assisted in bringing on your current miserable cold or flu.

We have so much to be grateful for but we take it for granted while also failing to show excitement for much of what we actually do realize that we are grateful for. Express it to the Creator with deep authentic passion and excitement by regularly offering thanks and praise.

Our Message to the Worlds

As we share our excitement with the world and with God, we must realize that our excitement and attitude and gratitude are being observed by others. When our joy shines through, it then has a profound effect on other people who want to also feel such joy.

When we send out a message through our expressions of joy, others will want to duplicate it in their own lives. And with this outward example we can bring more people into the Light of Truth. In the Bible The Christ talks about hiding our light, stating that "No man lights a lamp, and puts it in a hidden place, or under a bushel, but puts it upon a lampstand that others that come in may see the light". This is clear indication that the Light of Truth that flows out of us should be on a lampstand so that others may see it—*we* are that lampstand.

Allow your Light of Joy to be seen and shared and then you will find that your light can draw the right people into your life and cause the wrong people to flee from you. Our message of joy should be expressed to the world and to God, but we often hide our light and replace it with darkness. If all of mankind understood this then all wars would end and there would be no more bloodshed. We could take all of the billions and trillions of dollars spent on war and instead spend it on exploring the heavens, and possibly even visiting other worlds.

Is there other life out in the Universe? Some people find it hard to believe that there is life beyond our Earth and imagine that God only Created **us**, but this short-sighted view is nonsensical when you look at the views we have captured of the heavens. One of two scenarios is likely true: First, we might be the only real life in the entirety of the Universe, making us unbelievably special above all else Created. Or the more likely situation is that the Universe is teaming with life very similar to us and we are not worthy of ever going to another inhabited planet because we humans from our Earth would only cause even more bloodshed than we have here on our own Earth.

We will not be ready to truly explore the cosmos until we can live in our own world without killing our fellow man or believing lies. Until every last one of us has either died or learned to live in the full Light of Truth and allow that Light to flow out of us and shine so that others can see it, we are not worthy to venture out of our solar system. When we are of the Light of Truth then others can also come to that Truth and take of it to fill themselves, and again allow it flow out of them and shine for ever more people to see and do the same.

Let us all pray that we have the Light of Truth within us that we may draw others to the Light that someday, maybe, we will be worthy to shine that Light throughout the Heavens that other people may also receive it if they have not already. Give thanks and Glory to God.

Chapter 18

All that We Want

We all want many things, but few of those things are actually needed. We want good things and bad things. Some of the bad things that we want we already know are bad for us, but sometimes we might not realize that something is going to end up being bad for us. Even good things can end badly when we fail to use good judgement when using them.

Water is a classic example of something that is very good for us, but if we drink far too much water (gallons daily) then it can make us sick or even kill us because we wash critical nutrients out of our body by having far too much of it—yet without it, we die. Even something as good and pure and necessary as water has its limits.

There are many things in our lives that end up being bad for us; take the free-will of *choice* itself as another example. One of the greatest gifts we all have is our free-will. With it we can choose to do almost anything. But when we choose badly with our free-will, we then pay a great price. We want many things and with our free-will we choose from them and bring them into our lives whether it's something tangible or something we choose to do or say or believe. When we're unkind to others it's typically reflected back at us. The unkindness that we dish out to others is a choice that we make. The unkindness comes from something deeper that we actually want, but we are too blinded by our cruelty to understand this.

Knowing Our True Desires

There are so many things that we each want, and these *wants* come through our desires. *Desire* is a critical part of our humanity, and without it we would likely die. We can look at animals and assume that they have desires, but the actions of animals are more *instinct* than they are actual desires. The excitement that a dog has when its master comes home is somewhat more in line with desire than it is with instinct. While animals might actually have specific desires, our human ability to desire is far greater and closely replicates God's desire.

For the Creation that we now live in to exist, God must have had great desire and passion to take the time to figure out what needed to **be**. Our desires are modeled after God's desires in that they are articulate and vast.

When we have desires, often the desires that we have are not really of our own making. Many of our desires are induced by advertising or by seeing something someone else has. This does not mean that these induced desires are bad, but on our own we would likely not have come up with those particular desires. Who cares if the clothes we wore last season are "out of style"? Much of advertising indirectly tells us that what we have now is no longer any good and we need a new one. This invokes in us a sense of inadequacy and feelings of lower self-worth.

In our world of clutter and noise, we have all sorts of messages bombarding us with the "you're-not-good-enough" sentiment, which works well for the marketers. We emotionally buy into this message and it drives our *induced* desires. In many ways these are really *false* desires. Our *true* desires will come through the Light of Truth that we invite within us. When this Light is absent in us then our desires are really more along the lines of covetousness and greed that arise from lack of Light.

Let Us Gather Our Thoughts

True desires will be centered around advancement, exploration, love, and building up, rather than the typical tearing down of others or ourselves. Let's all gather our thoughts and consider what our true desires really are. Do we really desire the fancy car or home? Or is it something else causing us to want those things? This is not saying that wanting these things is wrong or bad, but rather we are trying to drill down to discover what *our own* **true** *desires* actually are.

If we allow ourselves to constantly be filled with the imagery that is called "advertising", then we have less room for our own true desires to grow and flourish within us. We can have both, but often our thoughts are so disrupted by the advertising and other temptations, that we end up never realizing our own true desires. When we quiet our minds and clear them, then we can focus more on our own *true* desires and keep them separate from the world's *induced* desires.

Gathering our thoughts and pausing to uncover our true desires allows us to pursue good things that we truly want, as well as pursuing our induced desires that in the long run do us no real good. When we're in the habit of quieting our minds and we do this for a number of years, it eventually all begins to show in the value gained in our lives by doing so on a daily basis at some brief point during each day.

The Right Time to Reap Your Harvest

As we navigate life and collect our things and eventually die, no one really cares much about what we had, unless it's cash.

Sometimes someone will want a particular valuable item or something that brings back fond memories. However, more often no one cares about the things we had, but they do care about how we treated them and what we taught them. Most of us have read obituaries that came across as very mean-spirited, but more commonly we read obituaries that praise the person because the deceased person was very good to people. There are also many neutral obituaries reflecting the feelings of those who wrote them.

We will always reap what we have sown and we need not wait until our death to reap our harvest. In fact, the only people who want to wait until death to reap their harvest are those who have sown nothing but weeds in their own life and in the lives of others. When we are not our best towards others, then those who can benefit financially from our death will often want nothing to do with that money or anything we had because they don't want those memories or contaminations in their own lives due the cruelty they experienced at the hand of the now deceased person. They just want to move forward in a life free of the torment that was inflicted on them by us while we were alive. Always check your own actions and thoughts towards others.

When you live a life guided by the wisdom brought through the Light of Truth, your wants and all of your desires will be affected by that Light. When you have chosen this path then the people around you will typically love you and trust you and will have only good and praise of you. This is a model of our Creator's desire, which is for us to love the Creator with all of our heart, mind, and soul.

The right time to reap your harvest is any time you do good, but there is no right time to reap when you have been selfish and cruel to others. You *will* reap what you have sown; there is no question about that. But *you* get to *choose* what you will reap. When you choose well by choosing the Light of Truth to guide you, then anytime is a good time to reap your harvest!

Our Joy is Righteous

There is a difference between *happiness* and *joy*. Happiness is derived from good things that happen which can be by chance; where on the other hand, joy is more often the result of making good choices and deliberately living a good life. When we have much joy in our lives because we made great choices and decisions then our joy is righteous.

With *happiness* it can't really be attributed to righteousness because we can be "happy" even if it's something bad that we are happy about. If we do wrong and steal from someone and then are "happy" that we now have the stolen item, then it cannot be considered righteous – ever!

With joy it is technically impossible to be joyful when we have cheated someone or when have cheated ourselves. Joy requires the Light of Truth which requires that we all be responsible for our own actions and the influence we have on others. We are *not* capable of staying in the Light of Truth and being bad at the same time. The moment the Light of Truth departs from us all of our righteousness then follows.

Plant only good in the hearts of others and allow them to see the joy that comes through the Light of Truth flowing out of you so that they may see that your joy is true and righteous.

What Do We Really Want?

Everyone really wants Truth and the Light that shines from it, but many of us have bought into the lie that has been presented to us that we are somehow not worthy as people to have that Light. We know that everyone seeks Truth because everyone wants the status that accompanies Truth. This is why we usually take a stand and demand that we are "right" about something that is being debated when we are actually not right or correct in any way.

Our desire to be correct and receive the recognition that goes along with *accuracy* is why we all too often have a near tantrum in effort to hide our own errors. Using our irrational reasoning, we somehow think that if we demand our way, even though we realize that we are actually wrong, others will *not* see us as the fools that we actually are. But those who observe our irrational behavior *do* see it and us as foolish when we do this. Had we chosen the path of Truth, then we would have actually been correct and accurate and would not need to demand that we were "right". There is nothing that will make something that is wrong somehow suddenly become right.

What we all really want is to be accurate and discover and learn and then share that learning with our fellow man, and this can only come through living in Truth. If you notice an ease in someone and that they seem to truly know a lot and are able to be helpful to you and many others, then the likelihood is very high that they have within them the Light of Truth. And they have probably been walking in the Light of Truth for a long time.

Chapter 19

Keep In Mind

Nothing discussed in this book will be of any use to you or anyone else if we cannot keep it in mind. Just consider the value of your ability to retain your past experiences. These past experiences include things we learned from others, things we discovered on our own, and any experience or input that has ever crossed our paths. But our experiences also include the thoughts we've had and things we have deduced.

There is still debate regarding how our memory is stored. Is the gathered information actually stored in the brain or anywhere else in the physical body? Or is the brain only an interface to our soul and our soul is actually what remembers things?

The Bible tends to indicate that our memory is a function of the soul or spirit, but "science" contends that memory is only relegated to the brain. It seems more likely that the brain is our soul's interface to the world and when something gets damaged in the brain then we are no longer able to recall those memories at will. But either way, our memory is important to us because it is how we learn and obtain wisdom as we filter our experiences through the Light of Truth. Our memory allows us to experience something today, and then tomorrow when a similar situation occurs we can draw from those past experiences to make better decisions. Drawing from past experiences helps us to decide our course of action based upon what we remember happening with the actions we chose to do during previous similar situations. We can then apply that knowledge to our new situation by taking a different course, thus causing us to be able to achieve a more favorable outcome.

If we didn't have this ability we would likely keep repeating our same bad choices over and over, continuously tormenting ourselves and only occasionally making good choices through chance. This is why disciplining children when they are young becomes so valuable to them when they are older; it gives them a foundation on which to build their lives and helps them to know a good path when they see it.

Retain Your Stores

We retain the experiences that we encounter throughout life. Sometimes these experiences are forgotten, only to pop into our mind when a particular memory is evoked from something we might associate with that memory, such as a smell or hearing a song. As we age and experience more and more in life, we can choose what many of our future memories will be by means of the choices we make as we are making new memories.

If we **do** a make a lot of foolish decisions, then we are going to have many more bad memories to recall in our future. When this is the case we tend to not want to remember those things, but suppressing our memories is generally not good. We are best served to deal with our memories both mentally and emotionally because, in truth, they will always be there, and ignoring and failing to deal with the pain that they dredge up will only cause that pain to come to us at a later date at the most inopportune times.

When we *properly* deal with painful memories it certainly can hurt to recall those memories, but there is no need to dwell on them and force ourselves to repeatedly feel their pain. Yet when we use all things for good, we can take those horrible memories and benefit ourselves with them. This is sometimes difficult to do when we have been treated very unfairly or have been treated in traumatic ways.

We have a "never-forget" attitude that permeates society, and it is not always taken as it is intended to be taken. When we "never forget" as a means of vengeance, then we are doing ourselves and the world a great disservice. However, we can and should retain recollection of traumatic experiences and then use our understanding to avoid, and help others to avoid, having to experience that same sort of trauma over and over again.

What we retain is not always bad. In fact, most of what we retain is typically mostly good. The good and the bad are both valuable to us as memories because we can base our future decisions and choices on those memories. Our good experiences can point us to what we should try to repeat in our lives. The joys and the pains that we experience will live on in our memories after they have moved on from our lives. We can try to suppress bad memories and work to recall only good memories, but all memories are retained and what we choose to do with these painful memories greatly affects and determines our future and our health. And for that ability we must be eternally grateful.

Remember the Reasons

Everything that you have experienced is tucked away somewhere in your mind with varying degrees of detail and recollection. When we recall any experience, we should also recall *why* it was a good or bad experience, because that is what gives us the ability to alter our own future. When we don't grasp why something was a bad experience, then we can't be very clear in knowing what to do or what not to do if a similar situation is presented to us. This is where the Light of Truth becomes the most important filter that we have available to us.

As we discern our history through the Light of Truth, we remember the reasons that a particular situation occurred and whether such situations were *just* and *true,* or if they were full of selfishness and deceit on our or anyone else's part. There are too many aspects to life to make one set of rules, other than Truth because Truth is critically important to us all. We can't really have some set pattern of what specifically is best. This is because everyone's life and circumstances are different, and only the standard of Truth can help each of us to navigate more safely through life.

We all must discern the reasons and then remember the reasons that situations occurred and turned out as they had. Those who take all of their life experiences and analyze and use those experiences and the analysis of the experiences for their own good and the good of others are typically the ones who thrive and have joy in this world.

Keeping Our Contents Clean

Our joy is increased when we have clean mental and spiritual contents. We may have lived a less-than-perfect life, but as previously mentioned, **we get to choose** if we will use our errors as learning tools for the benefit of our future, or if we will wallow in them and destroy ourselves by doing so. Too often we choose to wallow in our misery, or worse we create more misery by suppressing the memories and then we repeat the same errors over and over again that those memories could have prevented if they had been used properly.

Tough times do occur in most everyone's life, and we can take the memories produced during those tough times and clean them up to be used as lessons that can produce *good* by not allowing the same mistakes or conditions to occur again. Keeping our contents clean in this way allows us more protection and joy.

We also have *good* memories and experiences, and we typically enjoy indulging ourselves in those memories. Yet this too can become a trap for us. Good memories can be a safe place for us to recall, but if we refuse to move forward in life because the fond memories of our past are better than our current lives, then we have trapped ourselves once again and will struggle to move forward.

Keeping our contents clean is not about what you remember or how you remember it. Keeping those contents clean is about having the order in your memories that comes with Truth so that you can know and understand what was good and what was bad and then use that, at will, in your future when the need arises.

Keep your contents clean and orderly and thank God that you can go through your past and view it through the Light of Truth and come upon full realization of errors you have made and unfair things that have happened to you. You can also know and understand why something was *good* or *bad*, or *fair* or *unfair* when you use this gift.

Be Careful what You Store Up

Dredging up our past is not a particularly pleasant task, especially if there are many bad memories in it. We have no need to dwell on any unpleasant memories. When our memories are particularly unfair and painful it's easy to have feelings of resentment, bitterness, and unforgiveness. However, we must be cautious in not storing up resentment, bitterness, and unforgiveness because it tends to slowly and continuously eat away at us, and yet it has little or no effect on the person that was so cruel to us or who did us wrong.

Dwelling on past painful memories tends to work toward pushing us into unforgiveness. And storing up unforgiveness is a dangerous condition for us to be in. When we do this it leaves us ever bitter and resentful, thus inhibiting our own joy.

However, recalling bad situations for quick reference when similar bad situations present themselves allows us to avoid repeating *our part* of the circumstances that we found so painful the first time around. When we store up bitterness then we become blind to these valuable lessons, where instead we could have otherwise learned from those experiences.

Also let's not mistake unforgiveness for taking care to avoid those who continue to cause us unfair pain and conflict. The issues of differentiating *unforgiveness* and *common sense* are discussed in the books *Hot Water, Red Hot Marriage, Strong Family* and *Understanding Prayer*. Basically when we are already willing to allow someone back into our life who has repeatedly violated us, if they cease to violate us, then we have forgiven them. But to think that we must allow someone to continue to violate us *and* allow them back into our lives while they refuse to stop violating us has nothing to do with forgiveness, and it is a foolish thing to do so.

Do not store up unforgiveness and bitterness; instead store those experiences up as wisdom and understanding so that they become tools for your better future. We mostly focus our thoughts on our interaction with specific people who have caused us much pain, but the same applies to any experience, or memory of experiences that we had. We can even be bitter and unforgiving towards *ourselves*.

It doesn't matter what the situation or circumstances are, and it doesn't matter who was involved or even if no one was involved, the same will always hold true. When we keep our contents clean and we carefully store those memories as the learning tools that they are, we then make better choices and can carry that wisdom throughout our lives and share it with others who are struggling through similar troubles.

If there ever was a place to apply the lemons-to-lemonade thinking, it is in our memories of past hurts by turning them into valuable lessons. This alone is worth a lifetime of thank-yous to God.

Store Up Treasures

Yes, we can turn those old bad memories into treasures of wisdom for use in our future, but we also must take care in trying to store up *good* memories. In the Bible we are told to store up treasures in Heaven, but that is somewhat different than taking bad memories and converting them into lessons for good.

If we want to store up treasures in Heaven, those treasures are largely going to coincide with storing up memories that are actually good. We really don't have many fond memories when we or anyone else has been selfish. It is when we contribute to the good of the world and to the good of all people and our fellow man and to the good of our spouse and children that we build up our good memories.

We might have fond memories of past days of foolish behavior during our younger years, but if we are being honest then those years might have been "fun", but we probably did not truly experience *joy* at those times. And if in our mind we did elevate those memories to the level of joy, then we will be mistaken because foolish behavior cannot be "Treasures in Heaven".

Only through the Light of Truth can we begin to store up any treasures in Heaven. Our past mistakes are still mistakes and they are not "treasures in Heaven". But what we have learned from them, and the choices we make because of that learning and wisdom, can create treasures that we can store up for ourselves here on Earth in our mind and memory, as well as in Heaven.

We have been given a beautiful gift in being able to convert our darker personal times into points of light and then being able to discern and learn from those bad experiences in order to make great choices going forward—doing so builds up our treasures. And let us not forget that we can also learn from the experiences of others we observe when we are wise. For all of this we also must be eternally thankful to our Creator. You will make it through any tough times that you experience, and with the proper attitude those experiences will lead you to a better future.

Chapter 20

A Grateful Representative

As we live life, seldom do we stop to realize our purpose and our duties. Being a representative of God is not necessarily a required duty, but it is something that we all do regardless. There have been many people who have sought to represent God through preaching, or maybe becoming a priest who is dedicated to the service of God. Some of these people do a wonderful job of drawing others near to God, but not all do it well.

Over the years many people have turned away from God because of bad priests and preachers, and in a way it was right for some of those people to do so. You may wince at the notion of turning from God, but if those who "represent" God are leading us down a wrong path then we are far better off stepping aside. Sadly, we associate *bad* priests and preachers with God, which is utterly unfair to God. Just because someone claims they are, or present themselves as, "a representative of God" does *not* mean that they actually are. For instance, you cannot be for killing innocent babies still in the womb and then be expected to be taken seriously when you invoke God's name. And I dare say that those who do such will likely not have a happy end unless they promptly change their views—immediately.

God has nothing to do with foolish people using their gift of free-will to lead other people astray. Our life here is an important test of whether or not we are worthy for a good life beyond this life. We all have the ability to make the same sort of choices, and those choices can be good ones when we choose so. The choice for a preacher to be screaming fire-and-brimstone and shaming people for every little error may be accurate, but it is not always the best technique to draw people to the Light. What works to draw one person near, will not always work to draw others near.

A common problem with the church over the years was that priests were too uptight about the people's church-etiquette, demanding that they "act properly". Of course people should be paying attention in church, but if you want the churches filled, then do not condemn the congregation for their church-etiquette, especially the children; doing so will turn them away, as has been happening for many recent decades. A church should be filled with joy and thanksgiving, especially with regard to the little ones.

A grateful representative is not a priest that comes across to the congregation as "cranky" or "uptight". A representative who is grateful is you and I, or anyone else who has joy in their heart and is willing to share that joy with others. Do not let humans who claim that they "represent God" frighten you away from your salvation. When the Light of Truth gets too bright for them, they will flee if you stand steadfast in truth.

We all need to be the grateful representatives of the Creator so that when false teachers come along with their lies, then others can see the difference in Light and be drawn to the true Light of Truth.

What We Represent

We can be a grateful representative, but what is it that we represent? We are representatives of God, but that's more the way a person represents the company that they work for. Here we are referring to specifically *what* we represent, in that our body is indicative of something.

We are Created in the image of the Creator, and our likeness represents the various aspects of God even though God did not have a human body like ours when man was Created. The aspects of the Creator are things such as our ability to wonder and discern, and then to create. We have many aspects that are explained in more detail in some of the books previously mentioned. But just stop and realize that your body is "created in the image of". This means that every key part of you is an aspect of The Creator. Our body represents the very Creator that Created us, and a part of our quest is to explore this likeness. Doing so is the pathway that leads us to obvious conclusions.

If we choose to foolishly deny that the Creator exists, then we render ourselves unable to properly compare our likeness to God as we attempt to understand our origin and our Creator. Denying God is perhaps the most foolish of man's mistakes. As long as this truth stands before us every morning as we peer into the mirror and see our reflection and yet deny that we are of God, all hope is lost for us and we are technically unable to achieve salvation.

However, when we look at our form in the mirror and all of the intricacies within that form and then realize that it is representative of the nature of the Creator, it should invoke a great sense of awe and wonder in every one of us. What is the meaning of our hands and feet? What is the meaning of our arms or our legs? What about our ears and our eyes? What about our intimate parts, or our face that has so many capabilities, what does it all mean or represent in regard to the many aspects of God?

Thinking through what our bodies represent is an exercise that everyone should do, and is a book unto itself so we will not elaborate much on it here. Instead just take the time to consider both the male and female body and what the various parts and functions of those bodies represent regarding the aspects of the Creator. It is truly intriguing when you give it enough thought, and it is something that you can contemplate for many years, as it is a vast learning experience that can help you in your relationship with God and with man.

At Face Value

While our bodies do represent a great many aspects of the Creator, our face is particularly interesting with its eyes, nose, mouth, and even ears could be considered a part of the face along with the ability to sense touch with the face. We often associate touch with our hands, which is true, but *all* of our skin feels touch as well. This means that if we include the ears as a continuation of our faces, then the face contains all five senses of taste, touch, smell, hearing, and sight.

Regarding God there is something very special about what the face represents with the diverse and very powerful sensory input it has. We also have to consider the meaning of the output. We can speak and sing and express joy with our voices, but we can also communicate with our many facial expressions.

Our faces have such great value, yet we generally never stop to think about or appreciate it all. Take the time to get familiar with your own face and the expressions that can be made with it. Understand that your mouth is a complex loudspeaker that can share information, while at the same time it is also good for singing or enjoying a delicious meal that we work to prepare. Our teeth can chew food to better extract flavor and nutrition, and our tongue can taste food.

Consider the nose, it can typically determine between a delicious meal and the danger associated with different kinds of smoke or even spoiled food. And as spoken of in an earlier chapter, our ears can also detect danger.

Our eyes can see the danger of various kinds of smoke and quickly detect the danger level. Our eyes can detect danger in many ways but they can also detect beauty, giving us great joy!

When we feel the warmth of the Sun on our face or the cold of a winter sleet storm we can know how to dress. The face is really quite incredible. If we are not thankful for our individual senses, then we should at least be thankful for the face overall because without it, we would have very difficult lives.

More than any other parts of our physical bodies, the face is most representative of God. Take the time to think through your face and try to understand what each aspect of it means and represents in relation to the Creator in whose image we have been created. If doing so does not deepen your appreciation for God's great Glory then nothing likely will.

The Husband of Us

Our being "Created in the image of" does not end at our physical body. Our relationships are also "Created in the image of" our relationship with God. We are likened to a bride, with Christ being our bridegroom. The family model that we are all very familiar with is a representation of this bigger picture.

Far too many people could find this to be a discouragement in regard to God and Christ because they may have grown up in a fragmented or abusive family where divorce was involved or their parents were never married at all. Sometimes children in these families don't even know who their father is. There is also the added complexity of divorce and re-marriage where two families are blended. These human shortcomings are *not* a model of the relationship that the Creator desires to have with us.

The Creator wants us to all be a family that is faithful and true and dedicated to each other, rather than a family that has been fractured and has fallen away from each other. The view we have of a proper family where a man and woman meet and fall in love and stay together and then go on to have children that they love, is the model that most of us want to achieve. This desire is natural in us humans, and only our experiences and the surrounding society alters our desire for this. Most of us can change our attitudes and circumstances overnight when we choose to do so.

It is natural in us to seek steady relationships and have offspring, but the darker side of life tries to defy this and causes much pain for many of us. Generally, we develop an affinity for someone and we seek to be with that person, but our culture openly promotes infidelity and unrestricted premarital sex. When a couple is told that they have only a fifty-fifty chance of staying happily with the same person, it has a tendency to make them believe that marriage-for-life is only as good as the flip of a coin. But this is only true for those who go into marriage with the fifty-fifty mentality. Any marriage is going to only be as strong as the weakest person in the marriage.

Marriage statistics are discussed in the *Red Hot Marriage-Marriage Manual* in more detail, but our chances of having our marriage end in divorce are only as good as what we go into the marriage with. Additionally, your own marriage is not a fifty-fifty chance like statistics would have us believe, it is actually closer to two-to-one or two-thirds that *you will stay married*. Many people do have great marriages and have very good families that do resemble God's desired relationship with man. Our selfishness and our ability to harm others interfere with our design and the design we are meant to live by.

Just as a good husband will care for his wife and children, so too will we be cared for when we are faithful to God. If a spouse is not faithful and continues in being unfaithful, then there is little reason for the other spouse to stand by them. Yet, God has stood by the people and has given us all countless opportunities to stop our unfaithful ways. We truly owe many thanks to God for our continued opportunity to repent of our stupid and foolish behaviors and yet be accepted when we finally stop those foolish ways and ask God for forgiveness.

We Are In the Image Of

Everything about us and our bodies is representative of the Creator and our relationship with the Creator. In the more recent centuries the theory of us having had evolved has come to prominence, and in recent times is being forced on society like never before. Is this view correct? Are we just like the animals?

Everyone realizes that there are similarities between us and some species of animals, but do those similarities matter? And do the similarities "prove" that we are of the same biological lineage as some animals? This is where we often misunderstand our design and biology, which is elaborated on in a some of the volumes of the *The Science Of God* books.

Because we are so susceptible to *doubt* and *believing lies* we often follow fools and their theories. When we take time to notice as we're looking at any part of life, we see some very specific attributes, functions, and mechanics as at work. The question to ask is, do such similarities demand that two things are biologically related?

The idea that we have evolved is derived from nothing more than similarities that we have noticed between living creatures. But is a tire a descendent of a ball just because it is round? Or are they two completely independent creations? To go a bit deeper into organic living matter, did we evolve from trees because they too have limbs? And to go even deeper, we can look at all carbon-based life and ask if it all evolved from a single source, with both plants and animals being carbon-based life forms?

When you study design and engineering you will find all things that share similarities share those similarities because they work, not because one thing caused another. Buildings are built with cement, bricks, wood, steel, and glass not because they have evolved, but because those items work great for building buildings. So, when engineers *plan and design* a building they use those fundamental material building blocks. There are also aspects like doors, windows, walls, and roofs that are handy, so you will also find those in the design of nearly all buildings. Someone might consider these items and say that it's different because those items are not alive, which is true. But the problem with that argument is that we are not talking about the items specifically, we are talking about them in relation to their being used in a design because parts like windows, doors, walls, and roofs are universal as are the cement, brick, wood, steel, and glass that they are made with. Blood, bones, muscle, skin, and limbs are all universal building materials and parts that work well.

The fundamental design of many animals is similar to humans not because we evolved from or with them, but rather because their fundamental aspects are required to have a living being be alive. The first universal aspect of man is life itself, and in order to have living organisms in the animated part of Creation to actually be considered alive, that life has certain requirements. One of the requirements is to have a circulatory system. Another is to have some ability to latch onto things. Another is to consume fuels to power the body and pass nutrients to the various organs of the body. All of these things are universal parts, much like automobiles have universal parts. Some of the parts only work in certain models and other parts are more universal. This universal nature is inherent in all design that flourishes and is useful and can be seen anywhere. If we design something that has little or no universal purpose, then it will die out and no one will want it because no one will want to replicate it as it will be of little use them.

When a design has a universal nature it can thrive—life itself wants to live! What we see in nature is partially design and partially "evolution", but what we all too often miss is that we mistakenly assume that random-evolution is its own act when in reality it is a part of the obvious design. If design was so rigid as to only produce exact replicas then we all would look identical and there would likely only be one gender of each species then we would not have robin, sparrow, trout, salmon, oak, or maple but only bird, fish, and tree. In fact, if design was so rigid as to only produce exact replicas there would only be one "species" period based upon the notion of full-scope evolution.

This point of view can go on extensively, but for our purposes here you probably get the idea behind *design* and its universality. We are Created with design, and that design is based upon some of the most fundamental aspects of Creation and the Creator. We are indeed Created in God's image.

The Face of God

Elements of our Creation, like our body and the fact that we breathe, are all designed aspects of us, and those aspects represent various aspects of the Creator and of Creation. But perhaps the most interesting and the most powerful is our face. We each have a face and our face is representative of the face of God. What does each feature of the face actually represent? Think about each facial feature like your eyes, your nose, your mouth, ears, chin, even your cheeks and eyebrows, what do they represent?

Our faces are for communication with our fellow man more than any other purpose. Our face is our representation to the world. We are known by our face and it is our visual identity. Someone can see us a hundred feet away and realize it is us just by seeing our face at a great distance. Then when they approach us they can tell a lot about us just by the "look" we have on our face. At that point they can speak to us and we can listen to them and reply back.

Our face represents our *self*, and cumulatively we humans represent the face of God. This is why it is so upsetting to God when we are not living rightly according to God. Being thankful to God is important to us because it improves our disposition by making us better representatives of God. And the better we represent God then the more pleased God is with us, which can create even more joy in our lives, making us more thankful causing us to be ever better representatives of God and ever more thankful!

Chapter 21

You Are the One

You are important to God, and so is everyone else. There are many statements in the Bible that speak of our value to God. The Bible relays that if one sheep is lost then the Shepard will leave the larger group to go out to retrieve the one lost sheep. God wants every one of us to be safely walking in peace. But instead we all selfishly go off to do our own thing often causing ourselves unwanted trouble. In fact, most troubles are caused by us straying off course.

Do We See Anyone But Ourself?

As we navigate life, our *true desires* and our *induced desires* guide our way, but when those desires do not follow the Light of Truth they become very self-centered. As we rush down our paths in attempt to achieve our desires, we often find disappointment at the end of those paths because often it is only our induced desires that we are chasing. We're all in such a hurry to get to our destination that we fail to enjoy the ride, but we figure this out too late in life to be able to turn around and actually enjoy the ride. As far as our lifespan is concerned, we don't get "do-overs". Our lifetime is linear and no matter what we do, the clock keeps on ticking forward all the way to our earthly end.

Did you ever think what your dead parent, grandparent, or great-grandparent might tell you today if they could? Many would tell you that they lived wrongly and would change their ways and would recommend that you do so also. They would probably try to convince you to slow down and enjoy the ride as you ride along in life with those around you. They would probably tell you to take note of those around you and to enjoy their company. They would probably tell you to listen more to your children and spend more time with them and more time guiding them, and they would probably tell you to *listen* better to your spouse. They would probably beg you to change your ways so that you can be certain to avoid a dark end.

We hurry along and live to accomplish our induced desires but we fail to enjoy the ride as we selfishly reach those empty goals. And even when we are actually following our true desires, we often do so for only self-serving purposes. Most of us proceed with a what-can-*I*-get-out-of-this approach to life and we ignore that negative effect *our* desires might have on those around us. We become so blinded with our desires that everything else fades away. This ability to focus so intently on our work is inherent in our design, but we tend to use it recklessly.

We can follow our true desires, but if we fail to invite the Light of Truth into us then we are certain to follow those true desires selfishly, thus not giving any thought to other people. A true desire can always be used to benefit both ourselves and others for the good of man only when we are not doing so with only selfish motives. Selfish motives are borne of darkness.

We need to be thankful to God for the passions we have and realize that our intense focus is a powerful gift that must be used with wisdom, or it will end up hurting us and those around us.

You Are Relative

Who are you? Who are we? What is our purpose? We all feel, or want to feel, important. And to ourselves each of us is the most important person, but you are relative. To you the "you" that I am speaking of is "me". And there are many yous for you unless you are talking to a specific person. "You" can be *you*, or *you*, or *you*, as you point around the room. Gets a bit confusing doesn't?

Each one of us is both a "you" to someone else and a "me" to ourself. These directional designations are relative to who is using them and they change the perspective view of any discussion. *You* are a valued and cherished person to God and to others *if* you make yourself so. Stop to consider the detail with which each and every part of your body is made, and then think a bit deeper and realize that each part also has its parts that do amazing functions all without any effort on *your* part. To God you are special and only you can destroy that bond between you and God. "Me, Special?" you might ask. Yes, *you* are special to God, and the Creator does not want any Creation to be destroyed or dirtied in any way.

The Creator has gone to great lengths to make a place for you and it is up to you to keep that place clean and pure so that you have a great life filled with joy. Do not allow any of the other yous in the world destroy your "me". Be grateful for who you truly are and don't hide the true you. Realize that anything that is not of Truth cannot be the true you.

Never allow yourself to get caught up in "trying to be different" because then you're just like everyone else who is trying to be different, and the rest of us will notice the cheap imitation you have become in doing so. If Truth is not present in your life then it is almost certain that you are trying to be a cheap imitation of some other person, rather than the uniquely created you that you are supposed to be. Marking ourselves up with rebellion cheapens us a great deal and causes us to be inferior to all others who have not done so.

You are relative to others and you are uniquely Created in the image of The Infinite Creator. It is only when we are filled with the Light of Truth that our true diversity shines through for all to see.

There Are Others

Seeing others is often difficult for us as we obsess over our own desires, but there are others in this world whether we chose to acknowledge them or not. For every desire you have, most other people also have a desire. Consider for a moment that all of the hopes and dreams you have may or may not be shared by others, but every person has hopes and dreams of their own. That's a lot of hopes and dreams, and a lot of born-in desires. Be especially sensitive to your spouse's hopes and dreams as well as God's

This vast pool of desires, when they are true desires, must make God very proud as a Creator. The fact that so many people would desire good things and work towards following and creating those desires is an astonishing accomplishment! We are indeed Created in God's image, and in being like God in that way not only do we have our own desires, but we must come to the full realization that others have desires, and sometimes their particular true desire might be more useful than our own. Theirs might be better for the world and more urgent. What we miss is that often, or even mostly, our own desires *can* work harmoniously with the desires of others. We need to be aware that the actions of others are the result of their true desires, but *we often see the action as the desire* of what they are really seeking. Actions are *results* of desire, and discovering our own true underlying desire should be our goal.

It is when the true desires of two or more people come together in harmony that we see some of the greatest accomplishments occur in life. Being grateful to God for others and for their true desires and gifts has a tendency to bring those who can assist our own true desires across our own paths. Always be watching when you give thanks to God for the good that others offer the world.

Why Do We Not See Others

Even if we are thankful for the true desires and gifts that others have which with they contribute to life, and even if God has them cross our paths, we often don't see them because we are too focused on our own desires to notice them. This is like the "Red Car Effect" spoken of in *the Corner Stone books* where you simply do not notice how many red cars there are on the streets until you buy a red car of your own, and then suddenly you see red cars everywhere.

We get so wrapped up in our own tasks that we seldom take time to stop and look around to see *any* color car. As we drive the streets of life, all cars are *just cars*, but when we're looking for a certain color or brand, then they suddenly stand out to us. This same thing is true of other people. We are so accustomed to seeing people everywhere that we miss the ones that can assist our own true desires as we assist their true desires.

Many people have something to offer each of us. They might know someone who can solve a problem for you or someone who can give you some small piece of information that you're missing that will solve a problem and allow you to quickly advance. But we don't see or notice these people mostly because we don't consider that they too have true desires. We also don't notice them because we are too preoccupied with our own worries to see the solution that could be speaking directly to us.

It's surprising how common it is that we are simply too blind to see all of the treasures within people, including those we see on a daily basis such as our children or spouse. Tune yourself into the fact that all people have true desires, and some of those people's desires might require someone like you and your desires might require someone like them. Stopping to thank God for others and their desires assists us in being able to see more of the red cars in our own lives, especially the people that God sends our way to deliberately to meet our needs—Let's all stop to see and receive the hearts of others.

Kindness *To* and Love *Of* Others

When we're too busy with our own concerns we have this terrible habit of ignoring the rest of humanity. Yes, that's right; *there are **other** people* in the world besides any one of us. When we stop to thank God for the true desires and the gifts of others we tend to better notice other people.

We can't really offer much kindness and love to others when we're too busy thinking of our own problems because we immerse ourselves in our own lives and shut out the world around us. On occasion this might be needed when we have some difficult task that requires intense focus and a lot of our time. But the gratitude that we express to other people, and to the Creator for others, helps to make us more aware of them and their lives and struggles. When we fail to set our busy-ness aside, we also fail to show kindness and love to others. If you review your life, you will probably have a few fond memories that stand out. The reason that those fond memories stand out is because someone took the time to notice you in a special way.

Acts of kindness and love tend to stand out to those who receive them, becoming fond memories for them. *You* noticing others and offering kindness and love to them will become a fond memory for someone else. And when we do this, it opens us up to interaction, allowing others to offer acts of kindness and love to us, thus allowing them to become an additional fond memory for us.

It is the kindness and love that we all offer to each other that makes any relationship a good one. Kindness and love make the world a better place. When we are too absorbed for too long in any particular desire that we have, it tends to make the world and all of our relationships and interaction with others feel cold and uncaring.

Make sure to be thankful not only for your true desires and gifts, but also for others and *their* true desires and gifts. Express your thanks to God and you just might find kindness and love abound in your life when you're watching for it.

Chapter 22

To Question Why

Our desires, whether *true* or *induced*, are really a type of question that we seek to fulfill. But a desire is more of a goal that when answering many questions about, we are be able to actually achieve. Questions can be desires too because we want to know something. But a desire is something that is within us personally, where a question can be something that we must do that has nothing to do with any of our actual desires. In fact, it is possible that we sometimes must ask a question, yet we desire to not have to ask the question but we need the question answered for some unconnected reason, such as asking a question for someone who is not present so that we can relay the answer back to them. We also ask about things we know will have unpleasant answers, but that we must deal with as well.

Or when we ask a question we might be trapped in a classroom and ask about something that doesn't make sense regarding what the textbook says or something the teacher said that didn't make sense to us, but we really didn't care much about the topic and just wanted to make sense of what is being told to us. We also ask small-talk questions like "How are you today?" as we greet a customer, but too often we don't specifically really care how they're actually doing. This type question is only asked as a rhetorical greeting, and an answer beyond "Fine, and how are you?" is not really expected and usually is somewhat not needed. But we have another more interesting reason and way to ask questions.

The Gift of Wonder

Our ability to *ask* is the most important aspect of our spirit, and that ability really is actually our gift of *wonder*. Often when we ask "how are you doing?" it's really a rhetorical question that we're not really seeking an answer for. But when we are truly asking a question, then that question is provoked by our *wondering*. Our gift of *wonder* is a most magnificent gift to be thankful for!

The ability to wonder is strongly connected with our ability to imagine and foresee possibilities. Our curiosity is us wondering about something. "I wonder what's inside the box" or "I wonder what's out there", or "I wonder what will happen if..." Our gift of wonderment, together with our desires, is what allows us to dream up new and unique things—ideas that may never before have been made or even imagined.

When we see something, we might look it over and wonder what would happen if we changed *this* or *that* about the item. In wondering in this manner, we continuously create new and better things for the world. But just like God, when we create we try something and it might work well, but then we look it over and realize that we can improve upon it, and we can keep doing this and revising it until we have a perfect finished product that little or no more can be done to improve.

Our gift of wonder is so much more than only wondering how we can improve something, or wondering what's in the box, or over the hill, or on the other side of the wall.

How Did We Really Get Here?

We get to gaze at the Heavens and we are capable of wondering how we really got here and if we were Created. The Heavens are vast and there appears to be no end to what we see. We wonder how it all came to be, often looking to the Bible for answers. However, because of translation errors and lack of detail, along with our lack of understanding, we also look to science for answers to how it all came to be. But just as the Bible has translation errors, as explained in the book *Understanding The Bible* so too does science as revealed in *The Science Of God Volumes*.

When we read or see something, we have no choice but to do our best to interpret that information in order to try to understand it. When we do this we assume a meaning to the information, and if we then convey that information to others we will describe it the way *we* best understood it and do so in the best way that we are able explain it. Thus if we **mis**-understand something we will share that **mis**understanding when we relay to others what we have seen, read, or heard.

If we wonder how we humans got here and go on to seek answers to our questions by reading a poorly stated translation of the Bible, then we are very likely to get wrong information and misinterpret what actually occurred—the same is true of science. We can use our gift of wonder for good when we filter the information we receive through the Light of Truth and are careful in *not* making hasty foolish assumptions about the questions we asked.

Too often our gift of wonder is clouded by a particular bias we might hold, so instead of wondering fully and using sound logic and reasoning, we immediately make speculations and state them as if they are actual discoveries and facts. This is like if someone were to ask you how a simple spoon was made, and you, without studying it fully, made the assumption that spoons are *carved* out of metal. You could follow your assumption and do all sorts of studying and find all of the reasons why your theory is correct. But because almost all spoons are either *stamped* out of metal or molded with plastic, you would be wrong because you actually failed to *ask* any real questions.

As discussed in the *The Science of God Volumes* we likely are here because we were Created, rather than being a chance happening of some big bang and evolutionary process. But without asking enough questions, we come to very incorrect conclusions as we try to fulfill our induced desires, both scientific and Biblical.

Typically We Must Ask to Receive

When we study into a subject, such as Creation, we need to guard ourselves against making firm conclusions until *after* we have asked many questions and found solid answers. When considering Creation, there's a big difference between asking "I wonder how that occurred" versus "I wonder if it all exploded from nothing?" When we ask if it happened a certain way then we usually seek and accept only answers that will bring us to our induced desired conclusion.

If we ask how we all got here then we are not looking for answers to something unrelated like how many miles of roads are in our country. When we wonder how we got here we look for answers that pertain to that. The same is true when we ask if we got here through a big bang. For instance, when we do this we typically only ask questions that lend to our desired outcome of the notion of a big bang. This is not really asking, it is more in line with creating a path that we decided ahead of time that we want to be true. Unfortunately this method of reasoning is also common in our relationships.

So while we can ask a broad question, like "how did we get here?", we instead, all too often ask if it was done a certain way. In court this is referred to as "leading the witness" and is frowned upon by the court in any courtroom that has a *just* judge. When we lead the questioning in this way, we are really pushing for our desired outcome and it is a truly dishonest and selfish approach when we lead people away from truth.

Did You Really Ask?

Asking is fine, and without our ability to ask we would learn little to contribute to achieving our true desires. But did we *really* ask? When we ask with leading questions, it is similar to what the Serpent did to Eve in the Garden. But when God questioned Adam, God asked open questions and only asked for specifics after Adam stated the specifics.

We will receive answers no matter what we ask, but when we ask with leading questions, then those leading questions are intended to lead down a specific desired path. If you really scrutinize your motives you will probably come to a realization that you likely navigate your life using leading-questions to some extent. For instance, if we are on a budget and want to buy something, then the sentiment is often "We can afford this, right?", when the question should be simply "Can we afford this?" When we ask leading questions in this way it's not really "asking a question", it is more of a statement where we want someone else to agree with us to confirm what we want to be or imagine is true rather than what actually is true. This really touches on darkness because it almost always comes from selfish motives.

If you really ask a question in an open manner it's not going to be a leading-question or a statement-type question that allows only one predetermined outcome to be the correct answer.

Before Making Wise Choices We Must Ask

When we use leading questions as a guide to forge our paths in life, we lose all ability to be wise, causing us to encounter many problems due to our dishonest approach to life.

We must ask questions in a truthful manner if we ever want to know the actual truth. Truth is a tough topic for many of us to grasp because we miss that there is a difference between *Truth* and *what is true*. What is true is not necessarily of Truth. If someone lies about something, then it is true that they lied, but what they said was not true. We determine this through the process of Truth.

We need not look far to see people chasing the *status* that the wisdom borne from Truth brings. There are many so-called "experts" seeking the glory of the wisdom of Truth, but they don't have it so they pretend to have it by means of making leading statements that are designed to deceive and make them *appear* smart as they attempt to befuddled their opponents with such statements. When we choose this path, the frightening part is that often we don't even realize we're doing so because in school we are seldom taught to think things through on our own. Instead we are taught to repeat things other people want us to say.

To receive real answers that withstand the Light of Truth, we must ask questions that have no deceit in them and do not lead us or others to false conclusions. Real answers are received only when we ask questions openly and in the full Light of Truth. It is only then that we can make wise choices in anything we say, do, or believe.

When we ask "why?" or wonder how we got here, we cannot realistically expect ourselves to receive accurate answers unless we first seek Truth—It is only then that we will be able to discover the actual truth about something. Be grateful to God for your ability to seek Truth.

Chapter 23

Making the Choice

Asking questions and having desires are precursors to our making choices. In the last chapter we discussed asking *leading-questions* and living life in a *leading-question* way in attempt to produce our desired outcome. This should not be confused with our *true* desires and seeking a good path that will lead us to those *true* desires.

Of course we must do certain things to stay on our path, but before we take action to do those things we must ask ourselves questions, and if those questions are leading-questions then they allow us to deceive ourselves. Leading-questions have a specific design and intent to lead the person answering to a specific conclusion, or in this case it is better stated as *to a specific choice*. Discussions about a "specific choice" can be confusing because if you have a specific conclusion in mind and you chose that particular conclusion–then was it really a choice?

True choice requires free-will, knowledge, wisdom, and Truth. Without all of those, our choice loses its free-will nature and is no longer much of a choice *if* it can be considered a choice at all.

Leading questions work to strip us of our free-will-choice with an intent on getting us to believe something or say something that is not necessarily true.

True Choice is a Gift of Free-will

True choice is a gift of free-will and it is obtained through adherence to Truth. It is both a *right* and a *privilege*. Those leading-questions that we ask ourselves don't give us the choice that we believe we are making when we ask them.

Free-will is among the most valuable possessions we have, and with it we can choose Light or darkness. From a philosophical perspective, we often struggle with the notion of free-will because of our misunderstanding of statements in the Bible and our misunderstanding of the perspective that the statements are being stated from.

In the Bible it indicates that God knows what we are going to do, not necessarily specifically you or I in particular, but rather society as a whole. And whether it is us individually or as a societal whole, this foreknowledge of our actions is understood by many as "*predestination*". If everything is "predestined" it would mean that everything we do is predetermined and we have no choice but to do it, much like a robot. But this would make the notion of free-will irrelevant and the term free-will would likely not even exist because the concept wouldn't exist or be known to us.

The idea that everything is predestined is ignorant of many key points. One key point is that the idea of love could not exist because love is a free-will choice. Another point is that if God Created us in a way that we could not choose whether or not to love, then love is pointless because it would be like you setting up a bunch of robots and programming them to make loving statements to yourself, much like the false adulation obtained from many sources on the internet. The next key point is that it would make God out to be a fool, because why would you create something to do wrong and then get angry at that thing or person you specifically created to do wrong? The logic behind the idea of everything being predestined cannot even be thought of as childish because that would be an insult to all children.

The difference between a parent knowing that a child is going to almost certainly make an error, versus making certain that the child makes an error is worlds apart. God generally doesn't tell us what to do but rather tells us what we should do unless we are specifically in God's service as some sort of messenger, and even then, it was always optional for the person.

Our ability to *choose* is a gift resulting from our free-will which is a gift that is obtained through wisdom, and wisdom is obtained through the Light of Truth. When you consider the value of the chain of events arising from the simple action of inviting Truth into your heart, you begin to realize what a wonderful gift it all is and that we should offer much thanks and praise to God for *the gift of choice*. Always remember that this very same gift of choice is what allows someone to choose to love *you* of their own free-will.

Be Careful what You Choose

Free-will and the gift of choice that comes from it are very interesting. When we believe something that is untrue, it robs us of our free-will as long as we believe the untrue thing. As the lies of darkness and inaccuracy steal away our right of free-will, the darkness slowly tightens its hold on us until finally we enter into total darkness and deny **God our Creator** and we completely forsake the Spirit of Truth.

Be careful in what you choose because the choices you make today set your path for tomorrow, and the further down a wrong path we go then the more difficult it is for us to admit our errors and go back and change our ways. When we venture far down these dark paths there will be others who will try to keep us there and will not allow any Light of Truth to shine upon us.

Truth will always be the thing that darkness fears most, because when you are in the dark and any small glimmer of Light meets your eye, you are then able to move towards that Light to seek refuge. But if you don't act quickly someone or something will come along and block your view of the Light.

Our view is usually obscured by a lot of shouting and emphatic statements made by the keepers of darkness. We see this with news organizations reporting on politics where they refuse tell *all* of what is really occurring. They only show or tell enough to make it look like some innocent person did some horrible deed. Or worse, they make a *good* deed appear to be a horrible vicious deed. But they go further than that and actually make an evil deed out to be a good deed.

We also see the keepers of darkness doing this in regard to the Bible and Creation. In this case they create doubt in your mind by altering the words of the Bible and then take your doubt and increase it through manipulation of scientific facts.

Sometimes it only takes one seemingly insignificant lie or inaccuracy to move an entire nation into folly. When we choose to follow the inaccuracies of darkness it causes the Light to flee from our fouled spirit. We can believe that we are being truthful or believe that we are believing only what is true, but when we refuse to consider other opposing information then we have a problem and have trapped ourselves in error.

Our Choices Won't Change Truth

Truth is an interesting function that far too many of us don't understand. We hear the "this is my truth" or "that is your truth" nonsense often being vomited by the keepers of darkness, but that's an absolute perversion of the understanding of Truth. There is only ONE Truth and when someone says "that is your truth" their statement is actually pointing to their *opinion*, because what they are saying is that they hold an opinion that is opposed to the actual truth and defies the full process of Truth but they don't want to admit that.

Truth doesn't care what your opinion is, or what my opinion is, or what anyone's opinion is. Truth only concerns itself with things that are accurate, good, and true. You can demand that the Universe big-banged itself into existence all you want, but it won't make a difference as to what actually occurred during Creation. You can also add a few million dollars to your checkbook so that you appear rich, but unless you actually have the millions to deposit in the bank, your pretend millions are only *pretend* millions and will likely cause you to overspend if you're not careful, and banks do not take kindly of that.

No amount of screaming or shouting or demanding our way is ever going to change Truth. No matter how loud we are, or how sincere we are, or how impassioned we are, when we are wrong—then we are wrong. It doesn't matter if it is deliberate or if it is an innocent error—wrong is wrong. Lies are wrong, errors are wrong, inaccuracies are wrong, mistakes are wrong, and anything that is not of Truth is wrong. This basic truth will never change and it can *always* be relied upon. But be thankful for Truth.

We Are Illuminated When We Choose Rightly

For centuries people have sought to be "enlightened" through the notion that "knowledge" brings enlightenment, but most have failed to actually become "enlightened". This failure is often found in those who place "higher education" as their god. What many seekers of enlightenment fail to realize is that you can know the entire sum of all human knowledge and still be a fool, and a fool will *never* be enlightened. This was more difficult to prove before the technological revolution, but since the technological revolution has brought a great deal of human knowledge to the fingertips of nearly the entire world, we can now see and *prove* that—knowledge and access to it do **not** equal "enlightenment".

One could argue that educated people have the "knowledge", but that is not really completely true. The "educated" know that certain knowledge surrounding what they have studied exists and they may or may not have read it, although they might be able to look it up in one of the many books that they flaunt that sit upon their book shelves. This is no different than knowing something likely exists and then looking it up on the internet. In our modern times *everyone* has vast knowledge, yet many of us are still fools.

The illumination sought from the enlightenment era until this present day is now, and always has been, the understanding of Truth. Not what is true, but rather what Truth is. You cannot be considered "enlightened" without that basic understanding, and with it *anyone* can be enlightened. It is the Light of Truth that shines forth from those who have embraced Truth that causes us to choose rightly, and it is then that we are illuminated.

You can choose God and still not really be enlightened, and yet you can still be saved without being enlightened. Being saved only requires that love and kindness be in us and that we love others as we love ourselves while accepting that the Christ is the one who came for the Salvation of mankind. As long as we do not deny this Truth then Salvation is ours, but this is not the whole of being enlightened.

Enlightened is not lighting candles, or humming, or meditating or any other form of seeking to be enlightened. Not arrogance, demanding our way, flaunting our educated status, or any other such nonsense. Only the deliberate bearing of Truth can truly enlighten us. When the Light of Truth overflows in you and shines brightly, it is then that you are truly enlightened, and when you have achieved it you will know that the Creator exists and Created all things.

What Will You Choose?

Will you choose the false enlightenment of fools, or will you choose the true illumination of the Light of Truth? We can each wait to make this choice, but a day will come when it is too late. One of those possible times is when you die. Another is when the Christ returns as is predicted in the Bible and as is indirectly taught in many cultures.

The time is running out for all of us, and when it's too late, then it's too late. Heed the many warnings that we have been given and choose rightly.

In the book of Matthew, Jesus said "...Not everyone that says to me, Lord, Lord, shall enter into the kingdom of heaven: but he who does the will of my Father who is in heaven, he shall enter into the kingdom of heaven. Many will say to me in that day: Lord, Lord, have not we prophesied in thy name, and cast out devils in thy name, and done many miracles in thy name? And then will I profess unto them, I never knew you: depart from me, you that work iniquity..."

We have been given many such warnings throughout the Bible, both directly as the above warning states and indirectly in the examples set forth by the various peoples of the Bible. For this particular knowledge we must all be very grateful to God. We have been warned and can choose rightly *because* of these warnings. It is so easy for us to make that one single choice, in a moment in the blink of an eye, to embrace the Light of Truth and be eternally grateful to God.

Chapter 24

In It for the Long Haul

When we live life we often bounce around like a tennis ball being smacked back and forth as the players hit the ball to-and-fro. One day we decide *this* and the next day we decide *that*, and the next day we decide on *this* again. One day we have dedicated ourself to God, and the next we find an excuse to retract, and then on another day we become dedicated again.

The Christ talked about not being double-minded and about not being lukewarm. The Bible indicates that we would be "spewed out" because we were "lukewarm". Revelation Three says "But because thou art lukewarm, and neither cold, nor hot, I will begin to vomit thee out of my mouth. Because thou say: I am rich, and made wealthy, and have need of nothing: and know not, that thou art wretched, and miserable, and poor, and blind, and naked. I counsel thee to buy of me gold fire tried, that thou may be made rich; and may be clothed in white garments, and that the shame of thy nakedness may not appear; and anoint thy eyes with eye salve, that thou may see."

If you're going to get in it, then get in it and do so with passion so that you are not being double-minded. People wrongly think that if they go to church then all is well, but this is not true. I can only assume that God would like us to attend church, but with true intent rather than only out of obligation.

We need not become preachers, priests, or nuns to be in the service of God. Serving God can be done in all areas of life. And depending upon how you have been living your life, not much needs to change. Being in the service of God has more to do with your heart and your intent than it does anything else. And the easiest way to be in the service of God is to make your relationship with your spouse great, and together bring up Godly children.

If you are in it for the long-haul and you have the Light of Truth in you, then it will automatically be reflected in the way you live your life. You will also likely feel the passion in you, thus allowing you to avoid being spewed out with others who are lukewarm. Be in it for the long haul with passion and gratitude.

Our Oath is Our Promise

What is an Oath? What is a Promise? In some ways these two, *oath* and *promise*, are similar; but in truth they are very different. *Promise* means to send forth, usually being accompanied by some sort of agreement. When we *promise* something, we are sending out or stating our declaration that we will do, or not do, something. *Oath* is a bit different in that it is typically a promise sworn to in the presence of God, or in the name of God.

A promise doesn't carry much weight in value in comparison to an *Oath*. When we promise, we say that we won't do something again, or state that we will do something that we agreed to. But we typically can break that promise with little or no consequence. We might draw up some legal papers holding us to our promise, but it will have to be debated and decided in court whether we have actually broken our promise if contention should arise. We make lots of promises in life that we don't keep and often we never even intended on keeping them to begin with.

Sometimes our promises are explicitly stated as promises in words or in legal documents, but other times our promises are somewhat indirect, like when we make a statement with emphasis that we will be there at a certain time, but then we end up being late or not showing up at all.

Oaths are different and carry much more weight than *promises* do. When we make an Oath we are invoking the name of God whether we intend on doing so or not. In court we make a mild Oath but it's not really a full-blown Oath. In court when a witness enters the witness-stand they are asked "Do you swear to tell the truth, the whole truth, and nothing but the truth, so help you God?" to which we are intended to answer, "I do". It is succinct and direct and captures the essence of a desire for accuracy. But we are typically **not** allowed to tell the **whole** truth in court and so the "so help you God" part doesn't really make it an official Oath. An Oath must be expressed in the presence of God or with God as the one who will hold us accountable.

The level of accountability of a *promise* can vary greatly and is only dependent upon the level of agreement stated or implied. But the more weighty "*Oath*" carries with it the responsibility to honor our promise with potential ramifications of having to deal with God when we break that Oath. When we make an Oath God can become our best ally or our worst fear depending upon our actions regarding the Oath.

God is the first and the last, and the beginning and the end, and when we invoke the name of God we are putting God's reputation on the line in the eyes of others. God does not take kindly to us working to defame and foul the name of God. When we break an Oath that we swore to God, or by God, then we have committed ourselves to something very deep and meaningful. And even if we didn't really mean it, there still may be a price to pay for breaking our Oathed promise, but it's even worse when we actually mean it and then break the Oathed promise.

The general message here is that we shouldn't invoke the name of God if we don't really mean it. In the Bible's Matthew Five The Christ warns us about our Oaths and swearing saying "But I say to you not to swear at all, neither by heaven, for it is the throne of God: Nor by the earth, for it is his footstool: nor by Jerusalem, for it is the city of the great king: Neither shalt thou swear by thy head, because thou canst not make one hair white or black. But let your speech be yea, yea: no, no: and that which is over and above these, is of evil." This clearly tells us that we should keep the name of God out of our petty promises because those broken promises will backfire on us and cause us problems in our relationship with God when we do not, or cannot keep, them.

We should all be grateful that God is patient with us and our foolish actions, and we should also be thankful that we have been alerted and warned to not make Oaths that we cannot or will not keep. Thank God for the mercy bestowed upon us daily, and let us never make an Oath in haste or without truly weighing it on the Scale of Truth.

All Things Continue

When we make a promise in an Oath to God, by God, or in the name of God, we have to realize the severe importance of keeping that promise. Things of God are everlasting, and invoking God's name puts us in grave danger if we cannot, do not, or never intended to live up to our end of the Oathed agreement.

With the Creator being *the beginning* and *the end* and *the first* and *the last* we have to realize that the Creator's level of commitment to Creation is something that we cannot easily comprehend. When the Creator commits to something we can trust that it will be eternal if it was an eternal commitment.

Imagine making some sort of promise to a human king about something you will do for one of his children. What do we imagine would happen if that promise was broken and the child of the king was in some way harmed? In many countries the kings would think nothing of having us put to death.

Just like Creation has existed since it was Created, so do our Oaths. When we create an Oath by swearing to or by God we are saying, that in Truth we will abide by our Oathed promise. When we break that promise then we are attempting to defile Truth whether or not we intend to do so, and that is something that is unacceptable to God.

Our words live on and we must take care regarding when and how we use them. As a child you may recall reciting the phrase "Sticks and stones may break my bones, but words will never harm me." This is true when those words are said to you or about you if you disregard those words and move on, but it is entirely different when those words issue forth from your own mouth. Your words live on in the hearts and minds of those around you as well as in your own heart and mind, but those words live on in God as well, and when those words are not of Truth they attempt to foul God, foul Truth, and foul Heaven, and *that* will never be allowed. Trying to defile God or Truth could be likened to you trying to bust through a very thick concrete wall by running head first into it. You are not going to do it and you will get hurt or killed in the process—Truth is immovable!

The Eternal Promise

Truth is our eternal promised Oath from God. God's Oath is *the first* and *the last*; it is *the beginning* and *the end* and nothing can or ever will change that. As a technicality, I don't know that even God can change that because as far as God or anyone else knows there never was or ever will be anything or anyone before or after God. God's eternal promise is what holds the heavens in place. When the Creator's face is turned away from the heavens then the Creation we see with our eyes today will likely dissipate and dissolve into utter nothingness.

God's promises are all Oaths and are everlasting. Most of God's promises apply to all of mankind, but we must realize that when we defy *our part* of a promise made to us by God, then God is no longer obligated to keep the promise to us individually. This might sound as if God is breaking a promise, but that is not at all true. One could only view it that way if they were a keeper of darkness.

If God promises us salvation then that promise is eternal until it is fulfilled. But if the Oathed promise is conditional where we must do something before we die, then God has that clause in the promise that allows for the particular Oath to no longer be available to us individually. This is because we breached the one simple thing we had to do in order to obtain the promise.

Yes, all of God's promises are Oaths and they are all eternal, or they are for the duration of the promise that the time clause stated. But the one Oath that is most important to the entirety of humanity is the eternal promise of our Salvation. There are reasons that the *"chosen-one"* theme permeates nearly every culture of this world. All of mankind has been awaiting the "chosen one" since man's obtaining the knowledge of *good* and *evil* in the Garden of Eden. This is when God promised Adam and Eve that they and their righteous offspring would be saved when God would send his Word to save them. Without this Salvation through The Christ we would all be destined to hell. But through our gift of choice *we can choose* whether we will see Heaven or if it will be hell that we eternally dwell in, and for this choice we owe eternal gratitude to our Creator!

We often think of hell as an eternal punishment, and that may be so, but it also may be that there are only two choices and it is each one of us who gets to make the free-will choice for ourself. We have been notified repeatedly which one is the wise choice, and we have been warned repeatedly which one is the bad choice. Hell is more of a *consequence* of our own bad choices than it is a punishment from some cruel God. The Bible clearly states, more than once, that God prefers that *all* of mankind should see Salvation, but our nature foolishly resists that. Our thanks to God our Creator and to The Christ should be eternal because we get to choose the eternal Love and Light of Truth.

The Infinite Truth

Truth is infinite, for which we all owe a great debt of gratitude that should never end. Truth is living and it cannot be altered and it will never end. It is infinite and infinitely valuable. There is nothing we can do to defy Truth or change it. We cannot dirty it or hide it. Truth was there before we were born and it will be there when and after we all meet our end.

To live in an eternity void of Truth would be hell. Eternally realizing that we were wrong is something not one of us would ever want. Yet many of us are making that choice as we live our lives this very day.

If our souls live eternally no matter what we do, then in what state do **you** want to spend your eternity? Will it be in the state of darkness of hell that is void of all Light of Truth, a hell where we wallow in cold murky flames that emit no light and only absorb any remnant of Truth we may have in us so that it is hidden from our hearts?

Truth lives on with or without us and our troubles, and it will continue to live on because it is unchanging and everlasting and cannot be stopped. *We* get to *choose* if we will run with Truth or be run over by Truth. Truth stops for nothing. There is no amount of whining, or anger, or tantrums, or denial, or anything else that can change Truth. We *choose* Truth, or we deny it, and when we deny Truth **we** have damned our own soul. Thank God with passionate gratitude that you are able, on your own, to make the free-will choice of Truth.

It is Finished—To Thine Own Self Be True

We have come to the end of some of the many powerful things to be eternally grateful to our Creator for. As you consider all of the points made in this book, also consider allowing the Light of Truth to fully come into you. But *allowing* and *inviting* are two very different concepts. When we *allow* something, it means that we are not really an active participant, and what we allow can have a dramatic effect on our life. If what we allow into us is good, then good can come from it. But if it is bad then we will likely experience suffering.

When we *allow* something it can be bad, like when we allow someone to repeatedly violate us in some way. When we do *allow* that, then we will continue to feel the pain caused by the violation, yet we can choose to cast it out. The opposite is also true. If we allow the Light of Truth in us it will cause us to be full of the Light and experience Joy, yet we can also foolishly choose to cast that Light out of us.

When we only *allow* something, we merely let it happen, and if that which we let happen is the Light of Truth coming into us then the likelihood that we will eventually cast it out is very high.

It is when we *choose to **invite*** the Light of Truth into us that we will endure with the Light. To be true to yourself and to the God that Created you, you must deliberately choose to invite the Light of Truth into you. There are many preachers and priests that tell us wonderful things and call upon the name of the Lord, and yet they do not have the Light of Truth within them because some of them have only *allowed* the Light in, but they never ***invited*** it in with all of their heart, all of their mind, all of their spirit, and all of their soul.

Yet even *inviting* the Truth into you is not quite enough, nor is *allowing* it in us, because we really need to do both; and even doing both lacks determination. It is when we both *invite* and *allow* the Light of Truth into us **and then accept it** that we can retain it eternally. We can still reject the Light after we have invited and allowed it in us, but once we experience the Light and **accept it** there is little that will ever change our mind and cause us to reject it again. It is our final act of **accepting the Light of Truth** that makes the difference.

You, and only you, get to choose your final destination and how you will get there. Will it be a joyful trip illuminated by the Light of Truth, or will it be a tormented trip through many painful obstacles strewn about in the cold of the darkness?

Your true self is a reflection made in the image of God. To be true to yourself you must live according to your Created nature and *invite*, *allow*, and then **accept** the Light of Truth into you. True Salvation comes when we **invite** and **allow** and **accept** the Light that Christ brought to us when he said "It is finished" for which we all owe God our eternal gratitude!

It is Finished!
To Thine own self be True

Thank you, oh Wondrous Creator
We Bless you with our Hearts

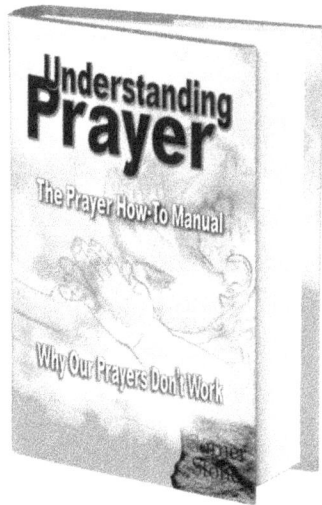

The Science of God Volume 1 The First Four Days

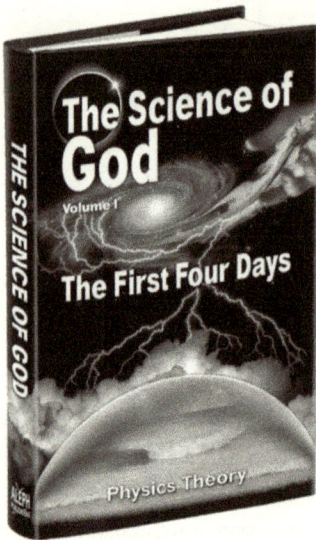

Volume 1 - The First Four Days

Is there a God? Did we evolve? Did everything start from a big bang? These questions have been plaguing our minds for many years. Only science-minded people and clergy seem to have the answers. But do they really have any true answers?

Is what we are told by science true? Is what we are told by the Church true? Or are there other better explanations for everything? Did we hitch a ride from Mars, or is that all fantasy science? Was everything created in six twenty-four hour days, or did it all take billions of years to happen? Few people are willing to even fully consider these questions, and even fewer have any coherent answers. *The Science of God Volume 1 – The First Four Days* challenges your current beliefs while asking tough questions of science and of the Church.

For years, Christian after Christian has attempted to argue for God and the Bible's Creation only to fail miserably. Why is this, why is it that Christians cannot seem to win this debate? Often Christians think they are winning the debate only to find themselves at a loss to answer the real questions, and then they get mocked for their poor answers.

Whether you are a scientist or an average Christian and want to discuss the Creation debate, *The Science of God Volume 1 – The First Four Days* is a mandatory read for you. *The Science of God* takes you through the thought process to enable you to speak intelligibly about Creation, the cosmos, evolution, and astrophysics.

**Search: The Science Of God Book
SayItBooks.com**

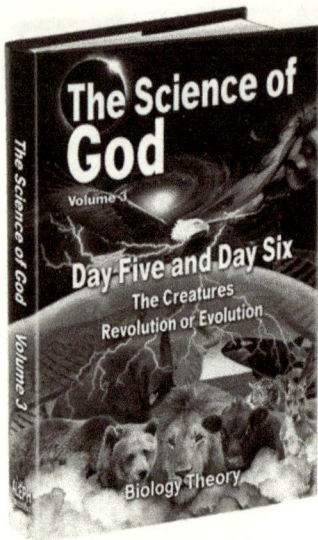

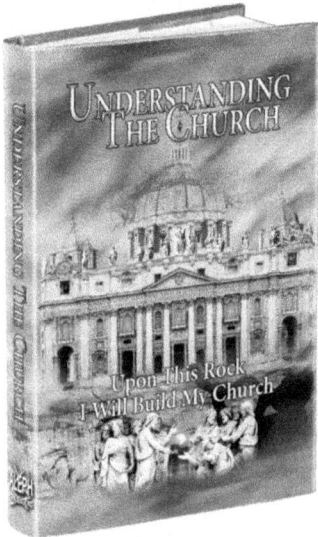

Notes

Notes

Notes

Notes

Notes

Notes

www.ingramcontent.com/pod-product-compliance
Lightning Source LLC
Chambersburg PA
CBHW051723040426
42447CB00008B/954